YOUR NAME OPENS DOORS

The Brand Worth System™

How Your Reputation Determines Who Gets Chosen, Trusted, and Given Opportunity Before You Speak

Thomas Wigington

QTR Foundry

Published by **The Foundry Press**
An imprint of **QTR Foundry**
Upper Marlboro, Maryland
thomaswigington.com

Intellectual Property

Disclaimer

Examples and Case Illustrations

Some examples in this book are composites drawn from recurring leadership patterns. Names, industries, and identifying details have been changed.

Cover and interior design by **The Foundry Press**

DEDICATION

To the people who shaped my path—the mentors who offered clarity, the colleagues who challenged me to grow, and the loved ones who believed in my capacity long before I did.

Your guidance, trust, and quiet acts of encouragement form the foundation of the leader I continue to become. This book is an expression of the lessons you planted, lessons I now hope to extend to others.

Thank you for lighting the way.

For Lt Col (Ret) Janette B. "Momma G" Goodman,
who first gave me the lens to see the difference between a career and a life. This book, and the work it represents, started with you.

To my mother, Vivian—thank you for the foundation, the values, and the steady belief that shaped the leader I continue to become.

In loving memory of my father, Thomas—your presence remains. You are carried in what I build and in how I lead.

To my brothers and sisters—Andre, Tamikeo, Quan, Quanet, and Carlos—thank you for the loyalty, the truth, and the bond that kept me grounded through every season.

In loving memory of my brother Adrian and my brother Eric—you are not forgotten. You are part of the strength behind everything I build.

To my teammates, past and present, and to the hundreds of leaders who have shared their journeys with me: the principles on these pages were not built in isolation. They were forged in the crucible of your real-world challenges and your hard-won triumphs. This book is my attempt to honor what you taught me.

And to my family—**my wife, Walia,** and our children: **Antoino (Latrell), Okayla, Ryan, Jamari, Tamari, Antavious, and Thomas III**—you are my daily reminder that leadership is not a role we perform at work, but a life we build in every moment. You are the joy, the purpose, and the *why* behind it all.

Finally, this book is for you—the reader who picked it up with a quiet desire to lead with greater purpose. For the leader you are now, and for the one you have the courage to become.

May you build a legacy that becomes your life.

Preface

Your Name Enters Rooms Before You Do

Long before a meeting begins, long before an interview or promotion conversation is called to order, something quieter is already happening. People are deciding whom to trust, whom to include, whom to watch more closely, and whose involvement will make the work feel safer to move. Sometimes those judgments are spoken aloud. More often, they happen in passing: a name offered as a solution, a hesitation no one explains, a quiet preference for one person over another.

By the time you arrive, the room has often already shifted. It may be a little more open to you or a little more guarded. The work may already be moving in your direction or away from it. What changed was not your résumé, your intentions, or even your raw ability. What changed was what your name caused other people to expect.

That anticipated pattern is what I call **Brand Worth**.

Brand Worth is not personal branding in the popular sense. It is not performance theater, image management, or the version of yourself you hope people believe. It is the working expectation attached to your name when other people have to make decisions involving trust, risk, responsibility, and opportunity.

I came to this idea by watching how organizations actually work: how trust forms, how hesitation spreads, and how certain names make movement easier before a word is spoken. That difference matters.

This book is about making that invisible system visible.

It is not a guide to seeming more impressive. It is a guide to becoming more dependable in the ways that matter most.

The work begins with a simple question: when your name enters a room before you do, what does it carry?

You may not control every room your name enters, but you can shape the evidence that arrives there first—and, over time, the weight your name comes to carry.

The QTR Foundry Leadership System

The QTR Foundry Leadership System is organized into four connected phases: **Intentionality, Reputation, Execution, and Stewardship**. Together, they describe how leadership matures—from self-command, to earned trust, to disciplined action, to multiplied value through other people.

Each phase answers a different leadership question, and each builds on the one before it.

PHASE I—INTENTIONALITY

On Purpose

Intentionality is where leadership gains direction. It establishes ownership, clarity, and disciplined decision-making.

PHASE II—REPUTATION

Your Name Opens Doors

Reputation is where leadership gains weight. It asks what your name has taught other people to expect. This book belongs to this phase.

PHASE III—EXECUTION

Running With Scissors

Execution is where judgment becomes useful action. It is the discipline of moving work well under real constraint.

PHASE IV—STEWARDSHIP

Stewards Not Gatekeepers

Stewardship is where leadership begins to scale. It extends standards, trust, and value beyond the leader's direct presence.

Taken together, these phases form the QTR Foundry approach to developing leaders who act with purpose, earn trust, move work forward, and build capacity in others.

This book focuses on **Reputation**—the phase where your name begins to shape opportunity, confidence, and access before you speak.

Table of Contents

Introduction

Your Name Arrives First

Your name does more than create an impression. It changes how much confidence, discretion, trust, and responsibility other people are willing to place in your hands.

That is the practical consequence of Brand Worth.

Brand Worth is not conformity. It does not require agreement, passivity, or risk avoidance. You can challenge assumptions, deliver uncomfortable truth, or pursue calculated risk and still reduce uncertainty when your reasoning is clear, the consequences are understood, your commitments are precise, and people know what happens next.

That standard is not reserved for executives. A frontline employee builds Brand Worth when a shift handoff is clean. An analyst builds it when a report can be trusted without rechecking every number. A coordinator builds it when deadlines and handoffs are managed without surprise. A manager builds it when the team knows the standard will hold under pressure. Title may widen the reach of your reputation, but it does not create the reality of it.

This book operates in the **Reputation** phase of the **QTR Foundry Leadership System**. Here, reputation is not cosmetic. It is operational.

Many people treat reputation as a side effect. They assume hard work will eventually become trust and that strong performance will speak clearly enough for itself. Sometimes that happens. More often, organizations are evaluating something more practical:

Does your name reduce hesitation?

People do not experience your intentions directly. They experience your pattern.

They remember whether they have to chase you, whether your communication arrives before a problem becomes a surprise, whether your tone stays disciplined under pressure, and whether you close the loop. They remember whether the work attached to your name tends to make the next step easier or harder.

Over time, those patterns become assumptions. Those assumptions influence decisions, and those decisions shape the opportunities, responsibilities, and trust that become available to you.

The model at the center of this book is simple enough to remember but demanding enough to matter:

Brand Worth grows through trust, consistency, and delivered results.

Trust establishes whether people can rely on your word and judgment. Consistency proves whether that standard holds across time, pressure, and changing conditions. Delivered results show whether the confidence attached to your name produces something the organization can actually use. Together, the three reinforce one another.

If trust is weak, the rest of the system is questioned. If consistency is weak, trust becomes fragile. If results are weak, confidence eventually stalls.

This applies whether you are leading a division, managing a team, running a project, covering a shift, serving a customer, or simply owning your work with discipline. The stakes may change with the role, but the underlying question does not: **what has your pattern taught other people to expect when your name is attached to the work?**

Everything that follows serves this system.

The Name Test diagnoses the expectation attached to your name. Trust, consistency, and delivered results build it. **Decision Space** shows what that expectation changes. Pressure, recovery, and communication protect it. Mentorship, sponsorship, and legacy determine whether it scales beyond you.

One of the clearest effects of Brand Worth is the way it expands or contracts Decision Space.

Decision Space is the practical range of trust, discretion, influence, and responsibility a person is allowed to exercise. Title matters, but title does not settle the question. Two people can hold the same role and still operate in very different realities. One is trusted to move independently. The other is watched more closely, asked for more proof, and given less room to decide.

The difference is often not intelligence or effort. It is confidence.

People who repeatedly reduce risk through judgment, reliability, and clean execution are usually given broader Decision Space over time. Oversight decreases. Opportunities widen. Others begin to trust not only what you can do, but what your name is likely to mean when the decision carries consequence.

At its strongest, Brand Worth does more than help a decision move. It can create Decision Pull—the point at which people begin seeking your judgment because repeated evidence has taught them that your involvement improves the outcome. Your name becomes part of the reason they want you in the work.

Decision Pull is not indispensability. It does not mean becoming the center of every decision or building a system that cannot function without you. It means your judgment has developed enough proven value that people seek it when the stakes justify the need.

That distinction matters because strong Brand Worth should increase organizational capacity, not create dependence.

This is why the book is about more than reputation in the abstract. Brand Worth shapes trust, and trust expands or contracts Decision Space. That space, in turn, influences the opportunities, responsibilities, and outcomes that become available to you.

Organizations do not distribute meaningful work at random. They place it where confidence feels justified.

That confidence can be earned in ordinary places.

A clear acknowledgment that gives someone a next-update time. A commitment precise enough for another person to plan around. A risk surfaced before the deadline instead of after it. A handoff that does not leave cleanup for someone else. A difficult message delivered early enough to matter. A mistake owned quickly enough that the problem does not become a trust problem.

None of those moments looks extraordinary by itself. That is part of the point.

Brand Worth is rarely built through one dramatic act. It is built through repeated evidence that becomes difficult for other people to ignore.

The same is true when Brand Worth weakens. One late update may not define you. One missed commitment may not change how people use your name. One poor response under pressure may be understood as an exception. But repeated often enough, small behaviors stop looking like isolated events and begin looking like a pattern.

Once that happens, organizations adapt.

They add checkpoints. They ask for more proof. They bring other people into the conversation. They narrow authority. They build protection around work they are no longer willing to trust without verification.

Sometimes that structure is called support. Sometimes it is simply risk management.

The opposite happens when the evidence is strong. People monitor less closely because they have learned what your pattern is likely to produce. They give greater discretion because they trust your judgment. They include you earlier because your involvement tends to reduce uncertainty instead of adding to it.

That is Brand Worth becoming operational.

Read this book as a mirror, not just a framework.

Each chapter gives language to patterns people often feel but do not always know how to describe. The workbook turns those ideas into evidence. Used honestly, it will help you see where your name creates confidence, where it still creates hesitation, and where your daily behavior may be teaching a lesson you did not intend to teach.

The point is not self-criticism. It is accuracy.

You cannot strengthen a pattern you refuse to see clearly, and you cannot build a dependable reputation by evaluating yourself only through your intentions or your best moments.

Begin where ambiguity enters your work.

Look for commitments that are too loose, communication that arrives too late, closure that remains implied instead of visible, and standards that shift when pressure rises. Look for places where other people have to chase, verify, interpret, compensate, or protect themselves because your pattern did not give them enough certainty.

Then choose one correction.

Communicate earlier. Make the commitment more precise. Close the loop visibly. Surface the risk before it becomes a surprise. Hold your tone when pressure rises. Make fewer promises and keep the ones you make with greater discipline.

Small corrections matter because Brand Worth is not built in speeches, intentions, or isolated peaks. It is built in patterns, and patterns repeated long enough become the meaning attached to your name.

That meaning carries consequences.

It affects whether people trust your judgment when conditions change. Whether your word can be used as a planning signal. Whether you are given enough autonomy to act without constant supervision. Whether your recommendation carries weight. Whether someone is willing to place their name behind yours. Whether the people you develop can carry the standard without waiting for you to enter the room.

By the end of this book, you should be able to diagnose what your name currently triggers, identify the behavior creating that expectation, and choose one correction capable of producing new evidence.

Use the book individually to test that correction through the workbook. Or use it with a team to establish shared language, identify where uncertainty is entering the work, and agree on one operating behavior to change together.

The goal is not to manage perception.

It is to build a pattern people can trust without needing you in the room to explain it.

Part I — Understanding Brand Worth

Part I begins with diagnosis.

Before you can strengthen what your name carries, you have to understand what it is already doing. Most people notice reputation only after something visible happens: an opportunity goes to someone else, oversight increases, a conversation happens without them, or their name seems to create confidence in one room and hesitation in another. Those moments matter, but they are usually evidence of a pattern that has been forming for some time.

That pattern is not limited to senior leaders. It forms around anyone whose work affects someone else's confidence: the person trusted with a customer issue, the analyst whose numbers do not need to be rechecked, the assistant whose follow-through keeps a team from drifting, the supervisor who steadies a hard shift, or the executive whose name makes a difficult decision easier to move.

Part I is where that pattern becomes visible.

Chapter 1 begins with **The Name Test:** what happens when your name is spoken and you are not there to explain yourself? Chapter 2 examines the **invisible environment** where those judgments form before official decisions are made. Chapter 3 shows how ordinary daily behavior keeps raising or lowering the value attached to your name.

The goal is not self-consciousness. It is accuracy. Once you can see what your name is already signaling, you can begin correcting the behaviors that create hesitation and strengthening the ones that create confidence.

Part I—The Standard

You are not evaluated from zero when you arrive. You are measured against the expectation your name already carries. To understand Brand Worth, you have to understand that starting point.

Chapter 1 — The Name Test

The decision looked sudden only from the outside. Inside the room, it had already been taking shape for several minutes. A deadline had moved up. The work was important. Whoever took it on would need to coordinate across teams, manage pressure, and keep several people from being surprised at once. In another setting it might have been a project lead, a shift supervisor, a client owner, or the analyst trusted to clean up a broken handoff. Here, it was a high-visibility assignment with little room for error.

Two names were under consideration. On paper, one candidate looked stronger. More experience. More technical range. The kind of résumé that often settles a conversation before anyone has to think too hard. But when his name came up, the room did not relax. It tightened.

No one questioned his ability. That was not the issue. The issue was the pattern attached to his name when pressure rose: late updates, tension that spread to other people, the sense that progress would require someone else to absorb the confusion around him. Capability was not enough to quiet those concerns, because by then the conversation was no longer about talent alone. It was about expectation.

"He is brilliant," one executive said, *"but when pressure hits, the work narrows around him. We end up spending as much energy managing the process as moving it."*

He was not in the room to answer for himself. His accomplishments were there, but they did not decide the moment. His name carried too much friction.

Then the other candidate's name was spoken. Her résumé was lighter. Fewer years. Less direct experience. And yet the room shifted in the opposite direction. People did not have to talk themselves into confidence. They seemed to arrive there almost immediately.

"She brings options when things get hard," another leader said. *"If she owns it, the work moves."*

She got the assignment because her name made the decision feel safer. One name caused the room to brace. The other allowed it to proceed.

That distinction sits at the center of this chapter. It applies far beyond senior leadership. The same test happens every day in smaller forms—in customer service, operations, project work, team coordination, and anywhere people have to decide whom they can safely depend on.

What the Name Test Reveals

The Name Test asks a direct question:

What happens when your name enters a conversation before you do?

Does the room become more confident because your involvement makes the outcome feel safer? Or does the conversation slow because your name introduces caution, explanation, or the need for backup plans?

That answer reveals more than perception. It reveals the operating environment your name has already created.

The question is not whether you are capable. The question is whether your name makes the next decision feel easier to make.

Patterns, Not Moments

Most people judge themselves by their best moments. Organizations rarely do. They watch for patterns.

A strong performance may draw attention, but repeated evidence creates expectation. Over time, people stop asking only whether you are capable and begin deciding whether you are reliable enough to build around.

That is why names are rarely experienced as neutral. They tend to land somewhere along a spectrum—from avoidance, where involvement feels too risky for the moment, to Decision Pull, where your name becomes a reason people want you involved. Between those points are hesitation, validation, and acceleration—each reflecting a different level of confidence in what your name is likely to produce.

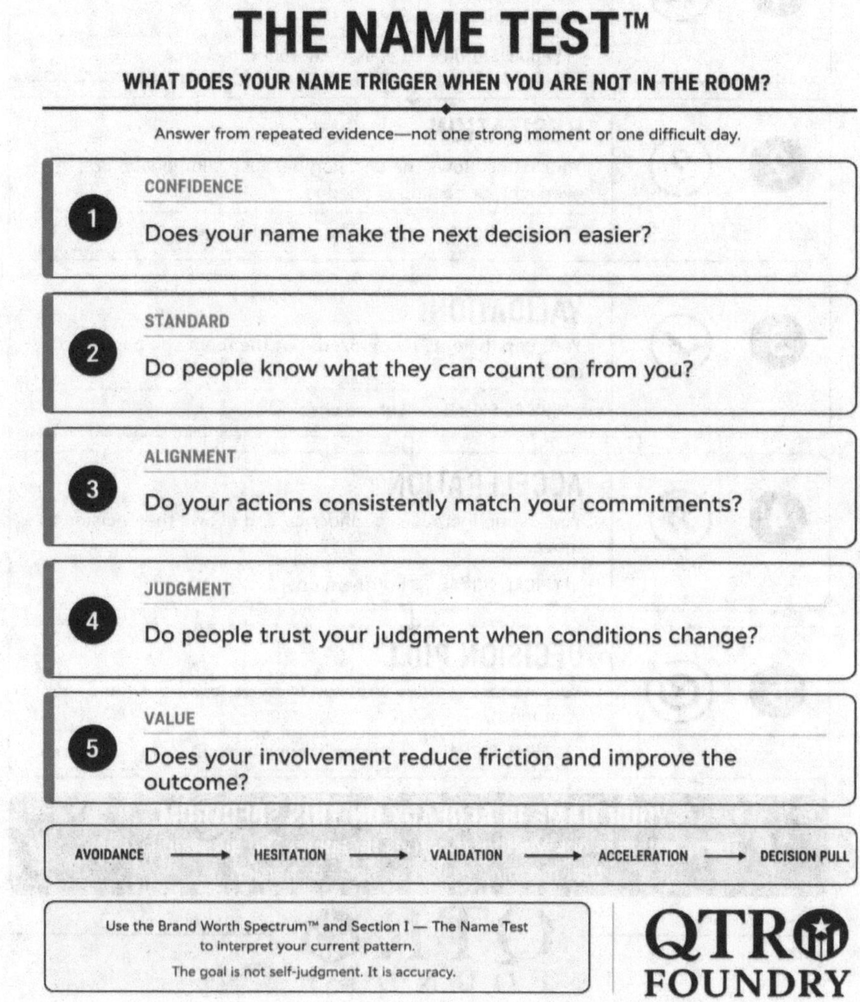

Figure 1 — The Name Test

What tends to happen in decision-making environments when your name is mentioned and you are not there to shape the conversation?

Figure 2 — The Brand Worth Spectrum

How is your name typically experienced when others are deciding whether to move, hesitate, or assign responsibility?

Acceleration and Decision Pull

Acceleration means your name helps a decision move. Decision Pull is different. Your name becomes part of the reason people want to move in that direction. They seek your judgment earlier, bring you into the work before the decision is fully formed, or ask for your involvement because repeated evidence has taught them that you improve the outcome.

Decision Pull is not indispensability. It does not mean being in every room or becoming the center of every decision. It means your judgment has enough proven value that people seek it when it matters.

Workbook Link

If you are working alongside the workbook, complete **Section I — The Name Test** before moving into Chapter 2. The point of this exercise is not self-judgment. It is accuracy.

The Standard

The standard is simple to state and difficult to earn: when your name is introduced, decisions should be able to move forward. At its strongest, your name becomes one of the reasons people want you involved—not because of title, visibility, or dependence, but because the outcome attached to your name is already sufficiently understood.

Your name rarely lands as neutral. Over time, people experience it as either a source of steadiness or a source of strain. What matters is whether your name makes the next decision feel clearer and more manageable—and whether repeated evidence has made your involvement worth seeking.

Chapter 2 — The Invisible Environment

Most people prepare for the visible room: the meeting, the presentation, the conversation where the decision appears to happen. They refine their points, think through their language, and try to make a strong impression once attention turns their way. That preparation matters. But in most workplaces, the decision environment begins forming earlier than that—and often in places you never see.

By the time you enter, people may have already compared notes, remembered a past handoff, recalled how you handled the last problem, or quietly decided whether your involvement is likely to make the work lighter or heavier. That can happen in a boardroom, but it also happens at a service desk, in a team huddle, on a project call, or in the hallway before someone assigns the next piece of work that cannot afford confusion.

What surrounds those visible moments is what I mean by the invisible environment. It is the place where your work is interpreted before you are present to explain it. It operates through remembered experience, side conversations, unspoken comparisons, and the quiet conclusions people draw about what your name is likely to require from them.

You do not shape that environment by performing harder in the visible one. You shape it more slowly—and more powerfully—through patterns people experience over time.

A Real Example: What It Looks Like in Practice

When Julian was hired as Director of IT Operations, he inherited more than a department. He inherited a pattern the company had already learned to distrust.

For years, IT had been experienced as a kind of black box. Requests went in. Updates rarely came out. Projects stalled without explanation. People had learned to associate the function with delay, silence, and frustration. By the time Julian arrived, that history had already begun attaching itself to his name.

His own Brand Worth was still largely unwritten. Most people did not know him well enough to have a strong opinion. But the department's history meant that neutrality did not feel neutral. The burden on his name was immediate.

He could have responded the way many leaders do when they inherit skepticism: with declarations, messaging, and promises of a new era. He could have tried to explain the future before giving anyone new evidence about the present.

Instead, he trained his team toward a steadier rhythm. They committed more carefully. They communicated earlier. When something minor happened overnight, he sent a short note before anyone had to ask what had occurred, what had been fixed, and what to expect next. If an update was likely to take four hours, the team committed to six and delivered in four.

None of this looked dramatic. That was part of its power. He did not try to outrun the old pattern with a large claim. He replaced it with dozens of small pieces of contrary evidence.

Four months later, the change became visible in a strategy meeting. A complex CRM integration was under discussion—exactly the kind of work that might previously have caused the room to tighten at the thought of IT owning it. This time, the CEO asked only one question:

"Who would run point?"

"Julian," the VP replied.

The CEO nodded and moved on.

The moment mattered because no argument was needed. Julian had moved, in the minds of others, from inherited risk to trusted execution. His name no longer required explanation. It carried enough clarity on its own.

The Environment That Actually Drives Decisions

The invisible environment is where behavior becomes pattern, and pattern becomes anticipation. It is where people decide how much confidence, caution, and access your name deserves before the visible conversation begins.

This environment lives in places most people do not see directly: the side conversation after a meeting, the memory of how you handled the last delay, the comparison between your handoff and someone else's, and the quiet question of whether assigning you the work will create momentum or more supervision. Those judgments are rarely announced. They are simply carried into the next decision.

That is why you are almost never starting from neutral when your name enters a conversation. Others are beginning from something already learned: an impression, a pattern, a prior inconvenience, or a remembered strength. That history may be thin or substantial, favorable or limiting, but it still shapes the starting point.

People often misread resistance as a response to the present moment when it may actually be a response to accumulated evidence from the past. The room is not always deciding who you are from scratch. More often, it is deciding whether what it already suspects about your name has been confirmed often enough to trust.

The Two Environments You Must Manage

Every professional operates in two environments at once.

The visible environment is where you present, explain, deliver, and respond in real time. It is where people can observe your performance directly.

The invisible environment is where that performance is interpreted, remembered, and converted into future confidence or caution.

Most people optimize for the visible environment because it is easier to see. They prepare for the meeting, refine the message, and try to perform well when attention turns toward them. That work matters, but it is not enough. A strong visible performance may win a moment. The invisible environment determines whether those moments accumulate into trust.

That is one of the hidden costs of being capable but unclear. Many talented people are treated like risk, not because they lack ability, but because their pattern is inconsistent enough that others cannot confidently build around it.

What You Control

You do not control when your name is mentioned, who is in the room, or what pressure surrounds the decision. You do control the pattern you create before that moment happens.

You control whether you close loops, communicate early, make precise commitments, surface risk before it becomes surprise, and keep your standard recognizable when conditions get harder. The invisible environment is shaped, little by little, by what you repeatedly make visible.

Once you understand that, your focus changes. You stop asking only how to perform in the room and begin asking what your name is already triggering before you enter. That question produces a different kind of discipline: earlier communication, clearer commitments, faster closure, and greater respect for the small behaviors that either reduce uncertainty or add to it.

Workbook Link

If you are working alongside the workbook, this is the place to complete **Section IV — The Reliability Loop** and identify where your pattern breaks most often: clarity, commitment, cadence, or closure. The point of the exercise is not to judge your intentions but to inspect your evidence.

The Standard

If your influence requires your constant presence, it has not yet been fully scaled. Your name should begin moving work before you arrive—not because of title or visibility alone, but because the pattern attached to it has already made the next step feel clearer and safer.

The goal is not to manage perception after uncertainty forms. The goal is to build a pattern strong enough that uncertainty has less room to form in the first place.

Chapter 3 — The Market Is Always Rating You

Most people imagine they are evaluated at recognizable moments: the review, the interview, the milestone, the meeting where feedback is finally made official. Those moments matter, but they are not the whole story. In most organizations, your value is being adjusted long before anything formal is said—and that adjustment happens around everyone's work, not only around people with senior titles.

An informal market operates beneath those formal moments. No one announces its prices, but names are continuously repriced according to what they signal about trust, usefulness, follow-through, and risk.

A teammate who always closes the loop gets priced differently from one who leaves cleanup for others. A technician who communicates clearly during a service interruption gets priced differently from one who leaves people guessing. A manager who surfaces risk early gets priced differently from one who lets problems arrive late. A senior leader whose name steadies a difficult decision gets priced differently from one whose involvement adds uncertainty.

You rarely see that mechanism directly. You feel its effects through earlier trust or cautious delay, broader autonomy or tighter oversight, momentum or resistance. The market adjusts before it ever explains itself.

What The Market Measures

Inside every organization, names carry value that is rarely named directly but constantly used. In that market, past behavior becomes present assumption. Every interaction adds evidence: how you communicate, follow through, handle pressure, close loops, and deliver. Together, those behaviors answer one practical question:

How much uncertainty does your name remove?

Micro-Behaviors Are Market Signals

Most people assume reputation is built in obvious moments: the major presentation, the visible win, the crisis everyone remembers. Those moments matter, but Brand Worth is usually built in smaller behaviors that repeat often enough to become expected.

A timely acknowledgment, a clear update, a closed loop, an early warning that risk is emerging, and a handoff that does not leave cleanup for the next person all teach people what working with you will require. These behaviors may look ordinary in isolation, but repeated over time, they become evidence.

That is the discipline many people miss: they wait for one major moment to prove themselves while the market draws conclusions from smaller signals every day.

Monday-Morning Standard

Start with one simple discipline: acknowledge every request with confirmation and a next update time.

A response such as, **"Received. I'll confirm by 3:00 p.m.,"** reduces hesitation immediately. It stops unnecessary follow-up, gives the other person a point of reference, and signals control without creating extra work.

Reliability often begins there—not with a major result, but with a clear response.

One vague update, delayed response, or quiet miss may not define you. Repetition does. Over time, delay begins to read as unreliability, silence begins to feel like risk, and inconsistency begins to invite oversight.

Silence deserves special attention because many people still treat it as neutral. In most organizations, it is not. You do not need perfect information to communicate. You need enough clarity to keep others from compensating for what they cannot see.

The Daily Pricing Mechanism

Every interaction either increases, maintains, or erodes the value attached to your name. A clear acknowledgment raises confidence; a visible next step sustains it; silence, vagueness, or an unannounced miss lowers it. These moves are small, but repeated signals become stable conclusions.

If you want evidence rather than abstraction, spend a week tracking three behaviors:

- Whether you acknowledged requests with a next update time
- Whether you communicated risk before the deadline
- Whether you closed loops visibly

By the end of the week, your pattern will be difficult to ignore. So will the places where your Brand Worth is leaking.

Brand Worth rises when you shift from occasional impressiveness to daily dependability. Organizations do not build around isolated excellence. They build around consistent certainty.

What Distinct Value Looks Like

That is also why your name must mean something specific. Generic reputations—solid, reliable, a good team player—may meet the bar, but they rarely give the room a clear reason to choose you.

Strong Brand Worth connects your name to a capability, a standard, and the felt experience of working with you.

Distinct does not mean flashy. It means specific, honest, and repeatable. When risk is high and time is short, organizations choose the person whose value is clearest and whose involvement removes the most uncertainty.

Workbook Link

Complete the **Pricing Signal Audit in Section III — The Brand Worth Equation.** Review three recent interactions to see what your behavior is teaching others to expect.

The Standard

When your name is mentioned, people should not need a briefing. Your pattern should already make what follows clear enough for the decision to move.

The work of leadership is to make that pattern worth trusting.

The Brand Worth System

Brand Worth rises when trust, consistency, and delivered results reinforce one another. It weakens when one breaks down. Figure 3 shows the system at a glance.

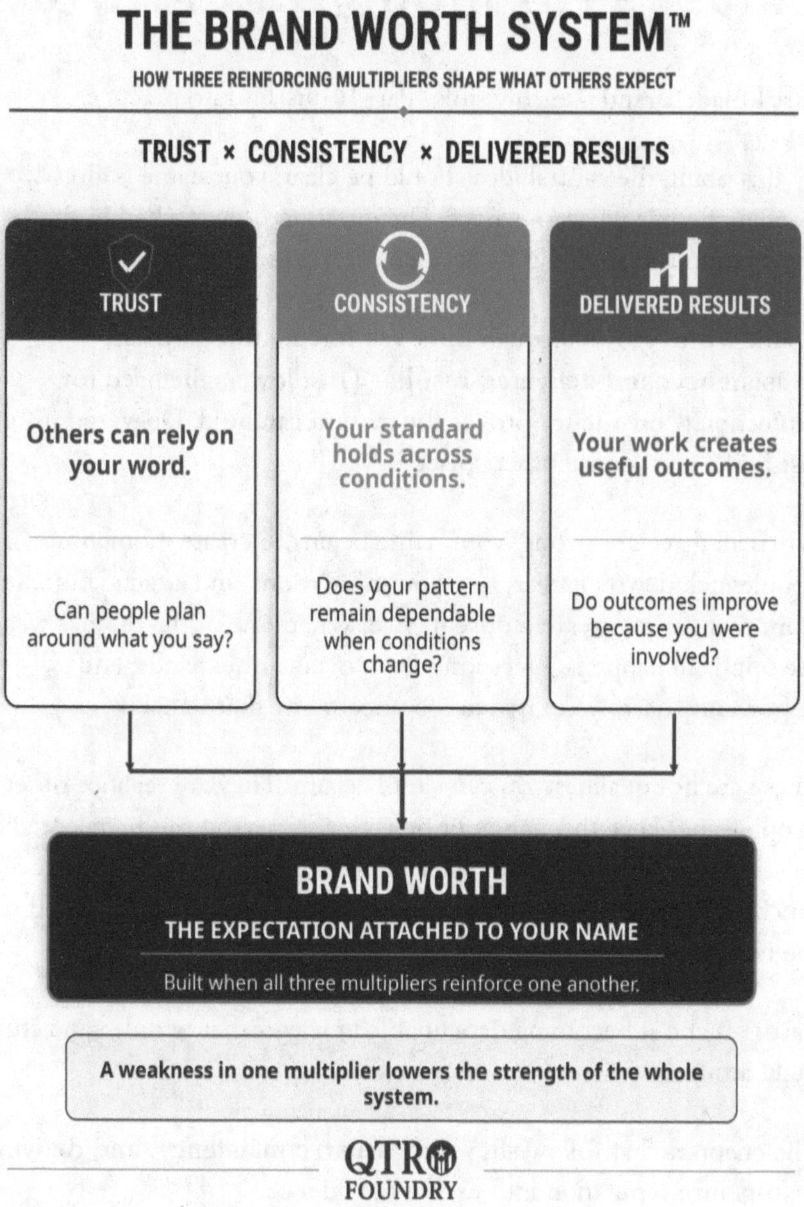

Figure 3 — The Brand Worth System

How trust, consistency, and delivered results work together to increase the value your name carries over time.

Part II — Building Brand Worth

Part I made Brand Worth visible. Part II turns it into practice.

By this point, the central idea should be clear: your name is already teaching people what to expect. The question now is whether that expectation is being built by accident or by discipline.

Brand Worth grows through three reinforcing forces: **trust, consistency, and delivered results.** Trust lowers the need for protection. Consistency proves the pattern can hold. Delivered results justify the confidence others place in you.

When all three are strong, your name begins to create momentum. People include you earlier, give you more room, and attach your name to work that carries greater consequence. When one of the three is weak, the opposite happens. Decisions slow, oversight expands, and opportunity narrows to match the uncertainty that remains.

These are not qualities you can simply claim. They are realities other people experience through your behavior. A person can be talented and still create uncertainty. A person can work hard and still require too much oversight. A person can deliver once and still not be trusted with the next important decision.

Part II is about becoming dependable in ways other people can actually build around.

The chapters that follow show how **trust, consistency, and delivered results** turn reputation into usable confidence.

Part II—The Standard

Brand Worth becomes stronger when trust is earned, consistency holds, and results arrive in a form the organization can use.

Chapter 4 — Trust: The First Multiplier

Trust is often spoken about as a virtue, but in working life it behaves more like infrastructure. It determines how quickly work moves, how much explanation is required, how much oversight gets added, and how much risk other people are willing to carry with your name attached.

When trust is present, people move with less friction. A supervisor can delegate instead of hover. A teammate can hand something off without bracing. A customer can believe the problem is actually being handled. A manager can give intent rather than detailed instructions. A senior leader can attach your name to a decision without needing a long defense first.

When trust is weak, the system compensates. More meetings appear. Validation expands. More people are copied. More checkpoints are inserted. The work still moves, but under protection, because doubt has to be managed.

That is why trust is the first multiplier in Brand Worth. Before people decide how much freedom, responsibility, or influence to place in your hands, they are quietly answering a more basic question:

Can we rely on this person when the stakes increase?

Trust Is Not Given. It Is Calculated.

People sometimes talk about trust as if it were granted once and then preserved by goodwill. Most organizations do not operate that way.

Confidence is recalculated continuously through behavior. People are always learning whether your judgment is sound, whether your word can be used, whether you communicate when conditions change, whether you follow through without being chased, and whether your standard still holds when the stakes increase.

Those are not philosophical questions. They determine how much autonomy others place within your reach and how much structure they build around your work.

If people trust your judgment, they give you space. If they do not, they add structure around you—what may be described as support but often functions as protection.

That distinction matters. Trust is not just about whether people like working with you. It is about whether your name lowers the amount of protection the system believes it needs.

Your Word as a Planning Signal

One of the clearest places trust is built or damaged is in the way people use their word. This is true whether the commitment is strategic or ordinary: a deliverable promised by Friday, a shift covered, a client updated, a report corrected, or a risk surfaced before it becomes a surprise.

In each case, someone else is planning around what you said. A loose commitment is not just a statement. It is a planning signal.

When your word is precise and your follow-through is dependable, trust accumulates quietly. When commitments are vague or unstable, people compensate. They check sooner. They copy more people. They narrow the room they are willing to give you.

That is how trust is often weakened in real work—not through scandal or dramatic collapse, but through the vague yes, the undefined timeline, the handoff nobody confirmed, the risk surfaced too late, or the promise made faster than it could responsibly be kept.

A trustworthy commitment names the deliverable, the timing, and the next update if conditions change. It does not create false certainty. It creates usable certainty.

A contract-grade commitment sounds simple:

"I will deliver X by Y. If anything changes, you will hear from me by Z."

That sentence is not bureaucracy. It is respect for the people building plans around your word.

Trust Expands Decision Space

Every professional works inside some version of **Decision Space**—the practical range of autonomy, influence, judgment, and responsibility they are allowed to exercise.

Trust is one of the strongest forces shaping that range. When trust is high, people need less proof. They monitor less closely. They allow broader judgment. They give more room to move. When trust is low, the opposite happens. Directions become narrower. Recommendations require more support. Decisions move around you or stop above you.

The difference is often not capability. It is the amount of risk others believe your name still carries.

This is the question trust is always answering beneath the surface:

How much risk are we willing to carry with this person?

The next two figures show how trust becomes operational consequence. Figure 4 illustrates how trust expands or contracts Decision Space. Figure 5 shows how that space affects execution and performance.

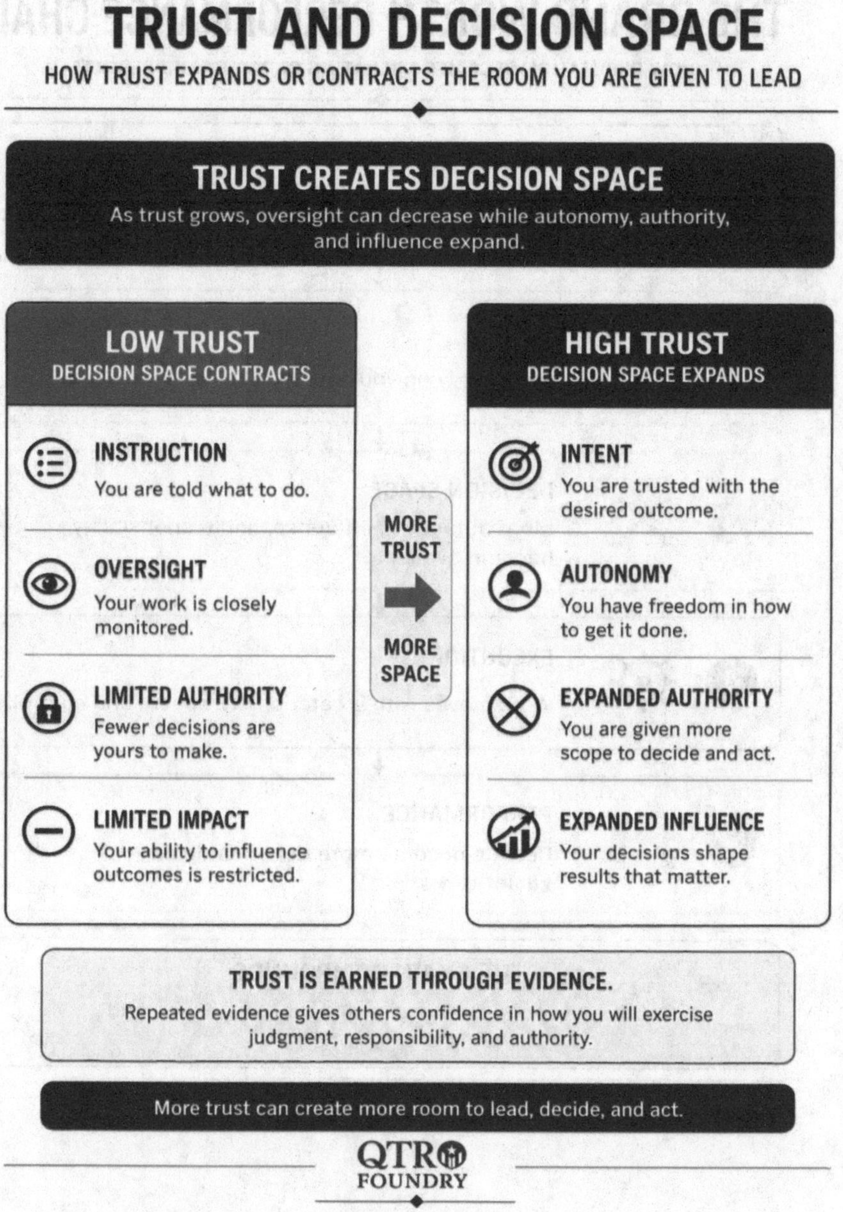

Figure 4 — Trust and Decision Space

How trust expands autonomy, increases influence, and determines how much risk others are willing to carry with your name.

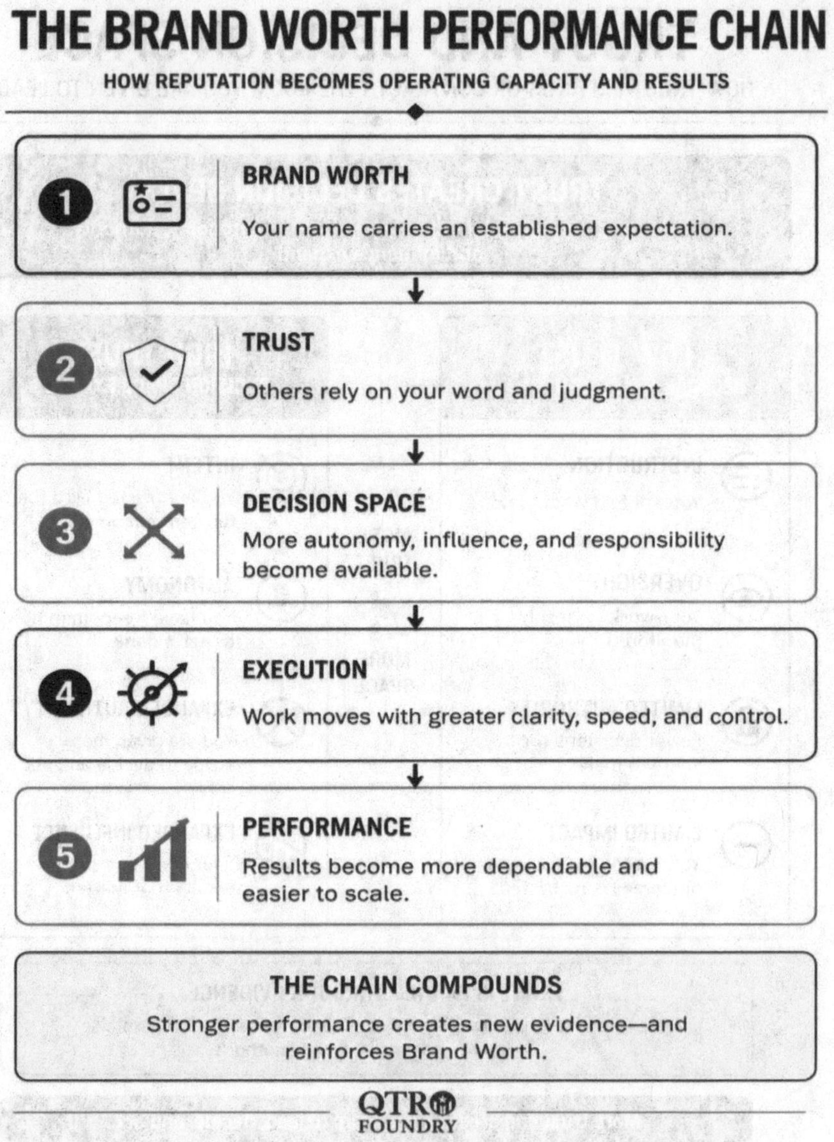

Figure 5 — The Brand Worth Performance Chain

Brand Worth builds trust. Trust expands Decision Space. Expanded Decision Space increases an individual's, team's, or organization's ability to execute and perform.

A Simple Example: Greg and Anita

Greg and Anita were regional sales managers facing the same problem.

A key component for the company's flagship product was delayed by a month. Both managers knew the delay would affect quarterly targets. Neither could fix the supply chain problem.

The problem was the same. The trust behavior was not.

Greg chose optimism and silence. He believed he could hustle his way out of the deficit. For three weeks, as the situation worsened, he told his VP, **"We're working a few angles. I'm confident we can pull it out."** When the quarter closed, Greg missed his numbers by 20 percent. The miss mattered, but the surprise mattered more. Greg had turned a business problem into a trust problem.

Anita made a different choice. The day she confirmed the supply chain delay, she sent a short memo to her VP: **"Due to the component shortage, my region will likely miss Q3 targets by 15–20 percent. We cannot outwork the lack of inventory. Here are the three steps my team is taking now to secure Q4 orders and reduce client churn while we wait."**

Both managers missed their targets. Their Brand Worth moved in opposite directions.

Greg's name became associated with unpredictable risk because his optimism outran reality. Anita's Brand Worth increased because her communication gave the organization usable reality while there was still time to act.

Trust does not require you to make every situation sound encouraging. It requires you to give other people reality they can plan around.

The Three Components of Trust

Trust rests on three reinforcing components: credibility, reliability, and integrity. Most reputational problems in organizations can be traced to weakness in one of the three.

Credibility — Do People Believe You Understand the Work?

Credibility is the first threshold. It tells people whether your judgment deserves weight. Competence matters here, but so do situational awareness, clear thinking, and the ability to interpret what is happening without being swallowed by it.

When credibility is weak, organizations compensate with validation. Decisions are questioned not necessarily out of disrespect, but out of necessity. Credibility gives people a reason to listen before you have to defend every choice.

Reliability — Do You Do What You Say You Will Do?

Reliability is where trust usually becomes real or begins to fracture. It is measured through follow-through, kept commitments, clear communication, predictable execution, and early renegotiation when conditions change.

Every commitment is a trust test—not only because of whether it is met, but because of what your handling of it teaches people to assume next time.

Reliability is not built by large promises. It is built by precise commitments kept repeatedly enough that people stop wondering whether you will follow through and begin planning as if you will.

Integrity — Do Your Actions Hold the Same Standard Under Pressure?

Integrity is what sustains trust when pressure makes compromise easier. It shows up in decisions made under strain, in ownership of outcomes, in the alignment between what you say and what you actually protect, and in your willingness to tell the truth when it costs you something.

Integrity is not proven by your stated values. It is proven by the standard you keep when convenience would excuse lowering it.

Without integrity, short-term results can still happen, but they begin to carry long-term risk. Organizations may continue using the person, but they add protection around them because they no longer fully trust the standard behind the output.

Trust Deposit Discipline

If you want to increase trust without increasing noise, focus on four repeatable deposits.

First, make fewer commitments and keep them relentlessly. A smaller number of kept promises is worth more than a larger number of unstable ones.

Second, renegotiate early when anything is at risk. If timing, scope, or quality changes, communicate before the deadline, not after it.

Third, close visibly with simple language such as **"Complete. Next step is..."** so others do not have to guess whether the work is finished.

Fourth, own the break plainly when something goes wrong: **"This is on me. Here is what happened, here is the fix, and here is what changes going forward."**

These deposits compound. They lower the organization's perceived risk and protect your name when pressure rises.

Workbook Link

Revisit **Section III — The Brand Worth Equation**, then use **Section VII — Communication Audit** to examine how truth, tone, and timing strengthen or weaken trust—and whether you close the communication loop visibly.

The Standard

Trust is established when your name gives other people usable confidence. The goal is not optimism that outruns reality, promises without proof, or confidence without follow-through. Your word should reduce uncertainty early enough that others can plan with it.

When that happens consistently, trust stops being a favorable impression. It becomes working confidence the organization can build around.

Chapter 5 — Consistency: The Proof Over Time

Trust may be earned in a moment. Consistency is what decides whether that trust becomes reusable.

A strong response can create confidence once. A clean delivery can make people lean in. A disciplined moment under pressure can change how others talk about your name. But organizations do not build around moments for long. They build around patterns they believe will hold tomorrow, next month, and when the conditions are less convenient.

That is why consistency matters so much. It takes trust out of the realm of impression and turns it into something others can plan with. It tells the organization that your standard does not depend on mood, visibility, convenience, or ideal conditions. That is what makes your reputation usable over time.

This applies far beyond senior leadership. A nurse builds consistency when handoffs remain clean across long shifts. A dispatcher builds it when updates stay accurate under pressure. A supervisor builds it when the team knows what standard will hold on a hard day. An executive builds it when judgment remains recognizable in more consequential decisions. Different roles carry different stakes, but the question is the same:

Does your standard remain dependable often enough for others to stop guessing?

A Real Example: How Small Promises Compound

Sarah did not look extraordinary at first. She was a mid-level logistics director with a reputation for being prepared, responsive, and difficult to surprise. No one described her as flashy. That was part of the point.

Her peers noticed the same pattern over and over. If Sarah promised an update by Friday at noon, it usually arrived before noon. If she saw a budget issue forming, she flagged it weeks early. If the timeline changed, she did not wait for someone to chase her. She said what had changed, what it affected, and when the next update would come.

None of those behaviors looked dramatic in isolation. They were small, disciplined acts of reliability. But repeated often enough, they began changing what her name meant to other people.

Six months later, the executive board needed someone to lead a high-stakes supply chain overhaul. The project was expensive, visible, and full of ways to create new trouble if the wrong person took it. The VP of Operations did not ask for a long candidate debate.

He said, **"Give it to Sarah. If she owns it, I know I do not have to worry about it."**

That sentence captures what consistency does. It allows a name to carry relief. It reduces the amount of mental and operational protection other people feel they need to add.

Sarah's Brand Worth was not built through one major win. It was built through the quiet compounding of everyday reliability until her pattern became safer to build around than the alternatives.

Why Consistency Matters More Than Intensity

Many professionals rely on intensity. They surge when visibility is high, work harder when pressure rises, and summon strong performances in moments that clearly matter. Sometimes that produces excellent outcomes. But intensity is not the same as consistency.

Intensity can win a moment. Consistency earns confidence over time.

One gives you a story to tell about what happened once. The other gives the organization a reason to believe the standard will hold again when it matters.

That distinction is easy to miss because intensity often looks impressive. Consistency often looks ordinary. But organizations rarely build around impressiveness alone. They build around people whose standards remain recognizable across changing conditions.

The Reliability Loop

I think of consistency as a loop: **clarity, commitment, cadence, and closure.**

- **Clarity** means the requirement is understood before the promise is made.

- **Commitment** means the promise is precise enough for others to plan around.

- **Cadence** means progress is communicated before uncertainty has time to grow.

- **Closure** means the work ends visibly enough that people do not have to guess whether it is complete or what comes next.

None of these practices are glamorous. Together, they create repeatable confidence.

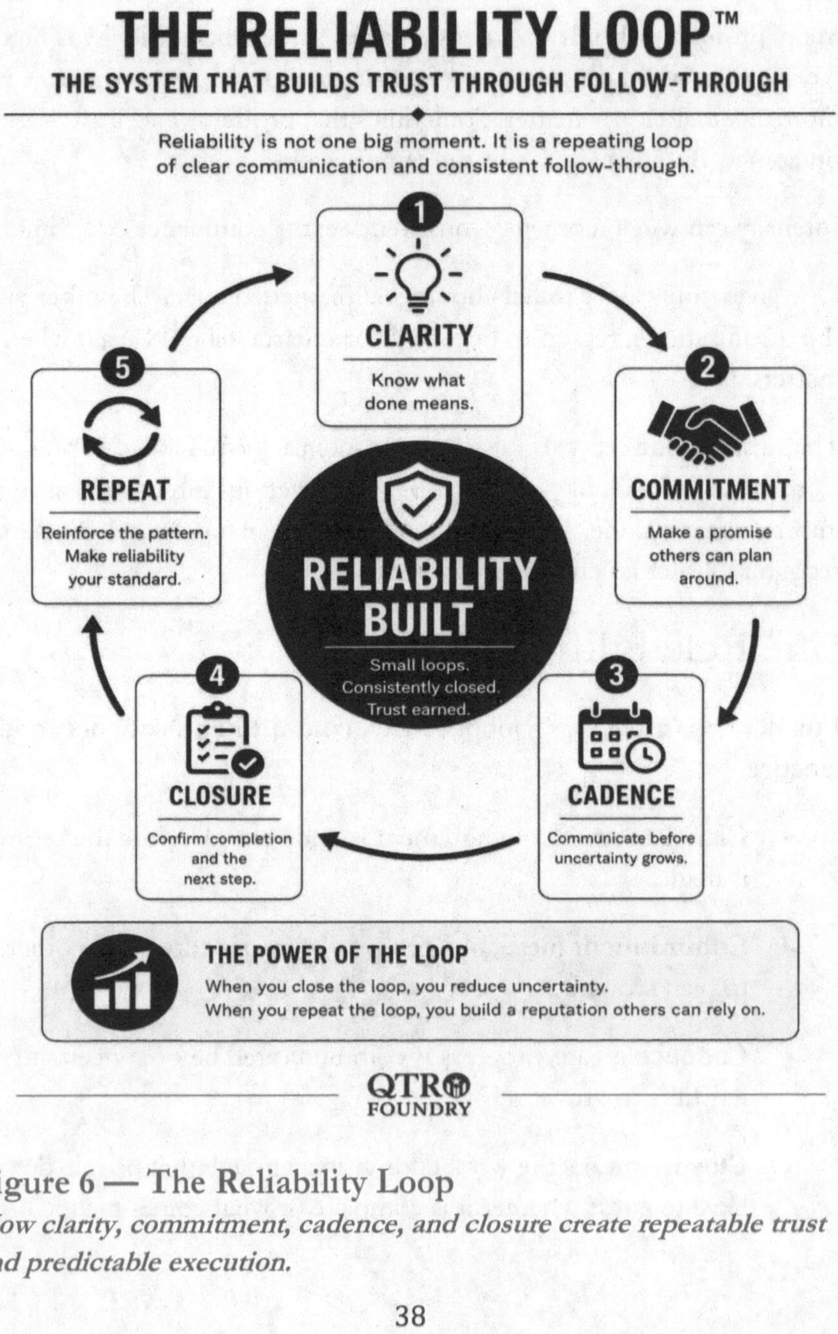

Figure 6 — The Reliability Loop

How clarity, commitment, cadence, and closure create repeatable trust and predictable execution.

Your Brand Is Your Floor, Not Your Ceiling

People rarely build trust around your best day. They build it around what they can count on when conditions change.

Your floor is the minimum standard others experience regardless of workload, visibility, or pressure. A high ceiling with a low floor creates variance, and variance makes risk feel harder to manage.

That is why organizations often choose the steadier person over the more dazzling one. Predictability is easier to build around than promise.

A high ceiling may make you impressive. **A dependable floor is what makes you usable.**

The Three Dimensions of Consistency

Consistency operates across three dimensions, and people feel the gap quickly when one breaks.

- The first is **behavioral consistency:** how you show up across environments.
- The second is **standard consistency:** whether your expectations hold when pressure increases.
- The third is **execution consistency:** whether your outcomes remain dependable over time.

Together, they determine whether others experience you as steady or variable.

Where Consistency Breaks Down

Consistency rarely fails all at once. It erodes through small deviations that accumulate into a pattern: overcommitting, communicating late, changing standards under pressure, letting tone become reactive, failing to close loops, treating exceptions as harmless, and allowing urgency to excuse poor execution.

Each deviation may feel manageable in isolation. Organizations do not evaluate in isolation. They evaluate patterns, and once a pattern forms, inconsistency stops being questioned and starts being assumed.

Why Consistency Compounds

Consistency changes how quickly decisions move around you. When your pattern is steady, fewer questions are asked, less validation is required, delegation becomes easier, and trust carries farther.

Trust produces belief. Consistency turns belief into confidence. Belief says you can do the work. Confidence says the standard is likely to hold again.

Organizations do not scale isolated belief. They scale confidence.

The Discipline Behind Consistency

Consistency is simple to admire and difficult to practice because the environment always offers reasons to drift. Urgency pushes people to overcommit. Fatigue lowers standards. Competing priorities weaken follow-through. Ambiguity invites delay. Pressure makes tone harder to manage.

None of those conditions excuses inconsistency. They are the conditions under which consistency becomes meaningful.

In practice, discipline looks ordinary: set clear standards, make fewer commitments, communicate before risk becomes surprise, protect your tone under pressure, and close loops visibly. These actions are not complicated. Repeating them when conditions become inconvenient is the discipline.

That repetition is what makes the pattern believable.

7-Day Consistency Check

If you want evidence instead of intention, spend the next seven days tracking three simple questions:

- Did I keep my commitments or renegotiate early?
- Did my standard hold under pressure?
- Did I close loops visibly enough that others did not have to guess what happened next?

The value of this check is not self-criticism. It is pattern recognition.

If you miss one, do not explain it away too quickly. Ask what caused the drift. Did you overcommit? Delay communication? Let tone become reactive? Leave closure implied? Accept work below your usual standard because urgency made it easier?

The point is not to defend your motives. It is to see what your behavior would teach other people to expect if it continued.

Workbook Link

Complete **Section VIII — Consistency Tracker**. Track whether you keep commitments, communicate before others have to chase you, hold your standard under pressure, and close loops visibly. Use the seven days to test one priority correction from the workbook.

The Standard

Consistency should make your name easier to trust over time. It should not depend on visibility, favorable conditions, or isolated strong moments. Your behavior should remain recognizable when priorities compete, pressure rises, and the environment becomes less convenient.

Trust may open the door once. Consistency is what keeps your name usable when the organization has to decide again.

Chapter 6 — Delivered Results: The Final Measure

Trust creates belief. Consistency proves the pattern. Delivered results are what make the pattern matter.

In the end, organizations do not operate on perception alone. They operate on outcomes. A trusted professional who does not deliver eventually becomes a concern. A consistent professional who does not move work forward eventually becomes expensive to maintain.

Brand Worth has to produce something usable. Results turn trust into evidence, consistency into confidence, and reputation into organizational value.

Results Define Reality

Many people are still judged first by visible effort: how hard they work, how much pressure they seem to carry, how many meetings they attend, how engaged they appear. Effort matters. But it is not the final measure.

Organizations do not build around how hard someone tried. They build around what changed because that person was involved.

The Difference Between Activity and Impact

One of the most common professional mistakes is confusing activity with results. Busy calendars, long hours, frequent updates, and highly visible effort can all create the appearance of progress. But activity is not impact.

Impact is defined by what changed:

- What moved forward?
- What improved?
- What risk was reduced?
- What decision became easier?
- What burden was lifted?
- What outcome was achieved?

A Simple Contrast: Brian and Chloe

Brian and Chloe were both ambitious mid-level managers. Both wanted to expand their influence beyond their immediate departments. Both wanted to be seen as ready for director-level responsibility. They chose different paths.

Brian focused on visibility. He scheduled virtual coffees with senior leaders, posted team wins on the internal company feed, and made sure his name was heard in all-hands meetings. He wanted to be known as someone with momentum.

Chloe focused on usefulness. She noticed a recurring data-entry problem creating friction between Operations and Finance. The issue was not dramatic, but it wasted time every week. Instead of talking about the problem, Chloe spent a Friday afternoon building a simple automated template that solved it.

With her manager's approval, she sent the template to the Finance leads with a short note: **"Noticed this was slowing both teams down. This may save your team a few hours this week."**

Six months later, the company created a new cross-functional leadership role. When the executive team discussed Brian, the feedback was polite but thin: **"Brian is enthusiastic and visible. I'm just not sure what he actually drives." His name meant friendly presence.**

When they discussed Chloe, the CFO spoke immediately: **"Chloe's template saved my team twenty hours last month. She understands how the business connects, not just her own function." Her name meant cross-functional problem solver.**

What Brian and Chloe Show Us

Visibility is not the same as value. Brian increased recognition, but he did not attach his name to a useful result. People knew him, but they could not connect his name to measurable movement.

Chloe did not chase attention. She solved a problem that mattered to people outside her lane. Her work reduced friction, saved time, and signaled business judgment.

That is the difference. Brand Worth does not rise because people know who you are. It rises because people can point to what improved because you were involved.

Results Are the Currency of Trust

Trust may open the door, and consistency may keep your name usable once you enter. Results determine how far that name will travel.

Without results, the value of your name eventually stalls. People may respect your intent, appreciate your discipline, and even like working with you, but organizations still need proof.

That proof does not have to be dramatic. Most results are practical: a decision made sooner, a risk reduced before it grew, a process improved, a customer protected, a team burden lifted, or a piece of work finished cleanly enough that the next step became easier.

Results create the evidence that your name deserves greater responsibility.

The Standard of Delivered Results

A result is not simply a task marked complete. Delivered results meet three standards at once:

- They matter.
- They meet the requirement.
- They arrive while they still have value.

If one of those breaks, the result weakens. A late result may no longer matter. A sloppy result creates rework. A polished result that solves the wrong problem creates noise.

Effective professionals do not just complete work. They deliver outcomes that are relevant, timely, and clean enough for the organization to use.

Results Under Pressure

Results carry more weight when conditions are difficult. Limited resources, compressed timelines, competing priorities, incomplete information, and increased scrutiny reveal whether a person can focus, prioritize, and execute without losing the standard.

Delivery is easier when the environment is favorable. Brand Worth rises when the standard holds and results still arrive when it is not.

Under pressure, results depend less on effort than on disciplined prioritization—deciding what matters most, what can wait, what must stop, and what cannot be compromised.

The Role of Prioritization

No role comes with unlimited capacity, which means results always depend on choice. People with strong Brand Worth do not try to make everything look equally urgent. They identify what matters most, protect the few outcomes that carry real consequence, and communicate clearly about the tradeoffs.

Poor prioritization weakens Brand Worth because it creates avoidable misses. People do not experience your internal effort. They experience what moved, what stalled, and whether you had the judgment to protect what mattered most.

That is why prioritization is not only a productivity skill. It is a reputational skill.

Clean Finish

One of the clearest differences between activity and delivered results is whether the work finishes cleanly.

A clean finish means three things:

- The requirement was met.
- Acceptance was confirmed.
- The next step was made clear.

Many professionals stop at completion and assume the rest will take care of itself. But incomplete closure leaves uncertainty behind. Others are left to guess whether the work is truly done, whether it met the standard, or what happens next.

That guesswork lowers the value of the result. Work that creates confusion at the finish line is not fully delivered, even if the task itself was technically completed.

A clean finish is one of the most practical ways to increase Brand Worth because it makes your work easier to build around.

Results That Travel

The most valuable results do more than solve the immediate problem. They travel. They save time beyond your team. They reduce friction beyond your lane. They make future decisions easier. They create confidence that extends past the moment of delivery.

That is one reason Chloe's example matters. Her result did not stay local. It changed how people beyond her own department experienced her usefulness.

Results that travel raise the value of your name because they prove your work matters beyond your immediate task list.

Workbook Link

Revisit **Section III — The Brand Worth Equation** and score your **Delivered Results** multiplier. Then use the **Clean Finish Standard** to review one recent assignment and close any remaining gap in requirement, acceptance, or next step.

The Standard

Delivered results should make your name more useful to the organization, not merely more visible. Effort matters. Intent matters. But outcomes are what give Brand Worth weight.

The goal is not activity that looks impressive. It is results that matter, arrive on time, and leave as little uncertainty behind as possible.

Results are the final measure because they prove whether trust and consistency have become useful to the organization.

Part III — Protecting Brand Worth

Brand Worth is not only built. It is tested, exposed, and either strengthened or weakened under strain.

Trust, consistency, and delivered results may raise the value attached to your name, but that value is never protected by theory alone. It is protected by how your standard holds when conditions become less favorable—when pressure rises, when failure becomes visible, and when communication matters more because uncertainty is already spreading.

That is the work of Part III.

Pressure reveals whether your standard is durable. Failure reveals whether trust can survive a miss. Communication reveals whether others can still rely on your judgment while the situation is still moving.

These moments matter because Brand Worth is rarely damaged by one imperfect result alone. It is more often damaged by what your behavior teaches other people to expect when the work becomes harder to carry.

Part III is about protecting the meaning attached to your name when conditions tighten.

The chapters that follow show how Brand Worth is tested under pressure, how it can be preserved through disciplined recovery, and how communication either stabilizes trust or weakens it in motion.

Part III — The Standard

A strong reputation is not proven only when conditions are favorable. It is proven when pressure rises, mistakes become visible, and your response still creates clarity, control, and trust.

Chapter 7 — Pressure: The Revealing Force

Pressure does not create your pattern. It reveals it.

When conditions are stable, many professionals appear reliable, composed, and clear. The deadlines are reasonable. The information is complete. The stakes are manageable. In that environment, weak patterns can stay hidden longer than they should.

Pressure changes that. It compresses time, raises visibility, limits options, and removes the space people often use to manage perception. What remains is the operating standard underneath.

That is why pressure matters so much to Brand Worth. When the work becomes harder to carry, people watch more closely. They notice whether you become clearer or more reactive, whether you communicate or go silent, whether your tone holds or spreads tension, whether you own the moment or transfer pressure to others.

Pressure turns pattern into evidence.

What Pressure Revealed

Marcus had built a reputation as a talented project lead. He was sharp, quick, and usually good in front of senior leaders. When conditions were stable, people liked having him in the room. He could explain complex issues clearly and usually had an answer ready.

Then a major client implementation began slipping.

The issue itself was manageable at first. A vendor delay created a two-week risk, and the team needed a clear response. Marcus saw the problem but did not want to raise concern before he had a solution. He kept telling the team, **"Let me work a few angles first."**

Three days passed. The risk grew. The team grew quieter. By the time Marcus briefed his director, the delay had already affected two downstream milestones. His update was polished, but late. The director's question was simple:

"When did you know?"

That question changed the room.

Marcus had not failed because he lacked intelligence. He failed because pressure exposed a pattern: he preferred appearing in control over creating control early. His silence forced others to absorb uncertainty he should have surfaced sooner.

A Different Response

David faced a similar situation two months later. A vendor issue threatened an executive-facing timeline, and the facts were still incomplete. David did not wait for perfect clarity before creating control.

He sent a short update to his director:

"We have a vendor delay that may affect the executive timeline. I am confirming scope now. Current risk is two to five business days. Options are: shift the internal review, add a second vendor for the affected workstream, or reduce the first-phase deliverable. I will confirm the recommendation by 3:00 p.m."

The issue still mattered. The timeline still changed. But David's response gave the organization something Marcus had withheld: usable reality while there was still room to act.

That is what disciplined pressure response does. It does not eliminate strain. It prevents strain from becoming surprise.

Pressure and Brand Worth

Pressure changes how behavior is interpreted. A delayed update that feels inconvenient under ordinary conditions feels like risk when the stakes rise. A sharp tone becomes part of the problem. A vague answer invites protection.

That is why pressure moments carry more reputational weight than ordinary ones. They teach people what your name means when conditions stop cooperating.

Brand Worth rises when your presence creates steadiness under strain. It weakens when your presence adds volatility, confusion, or unnecessary silence.

The Pressure Pattern

Everyone has a pressure pattern. Some people speed up before they think. Some go silent. Some over-explain. Some become sharp. Some overcontrol. Some avoid the issue until the consequences become too visible to ignore.

The question is not whether you feel pressure. Everyone does. The question is what your pressure pattern creates for others.

- Does it create control or volatility?
- Does it clarify the work or make people guess?
- Does it help others carry the moment, or does it transfer more weight onto them?

Your Brand Worth under pressure is shaped by those answers.

Figure 7 — The Pressure Response Model

How disciplined leaders create clarity, maintain control, and reduce uncertainty when pressure increases.

The Pressure Response Model

Under pressure, complicated systems are usually the first things to fail. That is why the response model in this chapter is simple by design:

Pause → Clarify → Prioritize → Communicate

Pause means controlling your first reaction before it becomes someone else's problem.

Clarify means determining what actually matters, what is known, what is unknown, and what risk is active.

Prioritize means deciding what must happen first, what can wait, and what should stop.

Communicate means reducing uncertainty for others before they have to chase clarity.

Together, these four moves create stability. That stability is one of the clearest signs of mature Brand Worth under strain.

Pressure and Decision-Making

Pressure makes decision quality visible. Leaders who maintain control usually make fewer, better decisions. They reduce rework, keep the team aligned, and protect attention for what matters most.

Leaders who react quickly without clarity tend to overcorrect, chase symptoms, and create confusion that outlasts the original problem.

Pressure does not remove your ability to lead. It reveals whether you can still lead without the comfort of ideal conditions.

Pressure and Trust

Trust is built slowly, but pressure tests it quickly. When the environment tightens, people watch three things closely:

- Your control
- Your communication
- Your ownership

A single volatile response can do outsized damage because pressure accelerates judgment. People may forgive the problem itself. They are less likely to forget that you made it harder to carry.

Repeated volatility changes how the organization uses you. Autonomy decreases. Oversight increases. Recommendations require more validation. Important decisions begin routing around you.

This is not always punishment. Often, it is risk management. If your name signals stability, you are trusted with more. If it signals volatility, the system protects itself from you.

7-Day Pressure Pattern Check

For the next seven days, watch how you respond to pressure in small moments, not only dramatic ones.

Ask:

- Did I pause before reacting?
- Did I clarify what mattered most?
- Did I prioritize what had to happen first and what could wait?
- Did I communicate the risk, the plan, and the next update before others had to ask?

- Did my response create control or volatility?

Then look for your default pattern. Do you speed up before you think, go silent, over-explain, transfer pressure to others, or lower the standard and call it flexibility?

Do not use the check to judge your intent. Use it to inspect the pattern your behavior teaches other people to expect when pressure rises.

Workbook Link

Complete **Section V—Pressure Response** and use the **Pressure Response Log** to capture three meaningful moments during the seven-day check. Identify whether your default response creates control or volatility and whether your replacement behavior changes the pattern.

The Standard

When pressure rises, people do not need a performance. They need a leader whose standard holds.

Your response should create control, not extra volatility; clarity, not noise; early communication, not silence; ownership, not deflection.

Pressure will always test your Brand Worth. What people remember is whether your presence made the situation easier or harder to carry.

Chapter 8 — Failure and Recovery

Failure itself is rarely the full problem. The greater risk is what failure teaches others when it is handled badly.

Every leader fails. Deadlines slip, plans break, assumptions prove wrong, and execution gets messy. No system is perfect, and no leader gets every call right. What matters most is what happens after the miss becomes visible.

Failure reveals more than the mistake itself. It reveals whether people can still trust your judgment, your ownership, and your standard once something has gone wrong.

That is why recovery matters. Failure may create the issue, but recovery determines the damage.

The Reality Most People Avoid

Most people do not lose Brand Worth because they fail once. They lose it because of what they do after the failure becomes visible.

They delay. They minimize. They explain before owning. They blame the conditions. They hope the issue resolves before anyone important notices.

That response turns a manageable problem into a trust problem.

The Moment That Matters Most

Failure creates a defining moment when the issue becomes visible. That is when people begin asking the question beneath every update, explanation, and corrective plan:

Can I still trust this person with responsibility?

They may ask it indirectly through questions about scope, cause, timeline, and next steps. Underneath those questions is a deeper concern:

Is this leader still safe with consequential work?

Two Types of Failure

In practice, most leadership failures land in one of two categories: **unmanaged failure** and **managed failure.**

The difference is not whether the outcome was bad. The difference is whether the response reduced uncertainty or expanded it.

Unmanaged failure delays truth, softens ownership, applies incomplete correction, and leaves others to guess what happens next.

Managed failure does the opposite. It creates control quickly enough that the organization can still trust the leader while the issue is being repaired.

A Simple Example

Dana led a small operations team responsible for monthly client reporting. One month, her team sent a report with an incorrect data field. The error was not catastrophic, but it reached a senior client before anyone caught it.

Dana could have slowed the response, investigated quietly, and hoped the client did not notice. Instead, she called her director immediately and said:

"This is on me. We sent the client report with an incorrect data field. The impact appears limited to one section. I am confirming the scope now. We will send the corrected version by 2:00 p.m.,

and I will add a second-person verification step before next month's release."

The corrected report reached the client that afternoon with a direct apology and no attempt to disguise what had happened. The client accepted the correction and moved on.

Dana's director did too, not because the error did not matter, but because Dana's response reduced uncertainty quickly. She owned the miss, contained the damage, and strengthened the process before confidence had time to erode.

That is what managed failure looks like. The mistake created concern. The recovery restored control.

The Recovery Protocol

When failure occurs, leaders need a repeatable response rather than instinct, emotion, or image management. Recovery works best when the sequence is simple enough to hold under strain:

Own → Diagnose → Fix → Guardrail → Close

Own the issue without delay or deflection.

Diagnose what failed, what allowed it to fail, and what standard was missing or weakened.

Fix the active problem completely enough that people no longer have to wonder whether it is handled.

Build a guardrail so the same failure is less likely to return.
Close the loop visibly so the right people understand the status, correction, and safeguard.

Those moves do more than repair the problem. They protect trust while the repair is happening.

Figure 8 — The Recovery Protocol

How disciplined leaders stabilize trust after failure by owning the issue, diagnosing it honestly, fixing it completely, building guardrails, and closing the loop visibly.

Why Ownership Comes First

Ownership comes first because it stabilizes the environment. People need to know who is accountable for getting the situation under control.

Clear language helps:

"This is on me. Here is what happened. Here is what we are doing next."

Ownership is not the same as absorbing blame for everything surrounding the issue. It means taking responsibility for leading the response without delay or deflection.

What Comes After Ownership

Once ownership is clear, diagnosis has to be honest. Leaders who reach too quickly for the convenient cause or the explanation that protects their image usually fix the wrong thing and leave the system vulnerable to repeat failure.

A clean diagnosis should answer:

- what failed
- what allowed it to fail
- what part of the standard was missing or weakened

From there, the fix must remove the active problem, not just quiet the immediate concern. Partial fixes extend uncertainty because people are still left asking whether the issue is handled.

Recovery also requires a guardrail—a visible change in process, handoff, decision checkpoint, communication cadence, or review step that makes the same failure less likely to return.

Finally, close the loop. Recovery is complete only when the right people understand the status, the correction, the safeguard now in place, and what happens next.

Forgiveness Capital

Two directors made the same mistake in the same week. Both miscommunicated a timeline to a key client.

The first director's manager called within an hour and said, **"Let's figure out how to fix this."** By the end of the day, there was a corrected timeline, a direct apology, and a plan. Nobody escalated. The mistake became a data point in an otherwise strong record.

The second director received a different response. His manager called too, but HR was included. A formal review followed.

Same mistake. Same company. Same week.

The difference was not the error. It was the account behind it.

Forgiveness capital is stored trust. It is the accumulated evidence that you keep your word, surface risk early, close loops visibly, tell the truth when it is uncomfortable, and improve what breaks.

Those deposits are made in ordinary moments long before failure arrives. Withdrawals happen the same way: surprise instead of warning, explanation instead of repair, silence when communication was expected, and blame when ownership was required.

Speed, Sequence, and Self-Protection

Speed matters after failure because the time between the mistake and the response becomes a signal in its own right.

A fast response stabilizes trust because it gives people control before uncertainty has time to spread. A delayed response erodes trust because it suggests you may not be willing to face the issue directly.

Speed does not mean rushing the fix before you understand the problem. It means communicating quickly enough that others do not have to fill the silence with concern.

Often the first message only needs four things:

- The fact that an issue exists.
- That you own the response.
- What you are confirming now.
- When the next update will come.

The order of response matters as much as the speed. Leaders often reach for explanation first because they want the failure to sound understandable. But explanation before ownership sounds like justification.

The sequence should be plain: own it, diagnose it, and explain only what helps others understand the risk and the response. Then fix it, guard against recurrence, and close the loop.

People may forgive the mistake. They struggle more to forgive the sense that you cared first about protecting yourself.

From Mistake to System Strength

Every failure contains information.

Handled correctly, it can become a process improvement, a communication upgrade, a clearer handoff, a better decision trigger, or a reinforced standard.

Failure is wasted when it produces embarrassment without improvement. It becomes valuable when it strengthens the system that allowed it to occur.

After-Action Note

After any miss, even a small one, write six short lines:

- What happened?
- What impact did it create?
- What was the real cause?
- What did you fix immediately?
- What guardrail now exists?
- How will resolution be confirmed?

Keep it brief. The point is not to produce a long report. It is to create ownership, correction, and confidence before memory turns vague and explanation grows self-protective.

Workbook Link

Complete **Section VI — Failure Response** using the six-line **After-Action Note**. Choose the recent miss that best reveals your default recovery pattern—not the safest example.

The Standard

When something breaks, your response should create stability.

Silence creates doubt, excuses erode trust, and partial correction leaves people guessing. Recovery requires disciplined ownership: own the issue, diagnose it honestly, fix it completely, build a guardrail, and close the loop visibly.

Failure will always test Brand Worth. Recovery is what decides what people remember.

Chapter 9 — Communication: Truth, Tone, and Timing

Communication is not secondary to leadership. In many moments, it is the form leadership takes.

People may not see every decision you make or understand every constraint you are carrying. They may not know the tradeoffs behind the work or the pressure shaping the day. But they experience your communication immediately, and that experience becomes evidence.

It tells them whether you are clear or vague, early or late, controlled or reactive, honest or softened, present or silent. Over time, those signals become part of your Brand Worth.

The Role Communication Actually Plays

Most people treat communication as a support function—something that explains the work once the important decisions have already been made.

In real organizational life, communication often does far more than explain. It controls how much certainty, trust, and alignment exist while the work is still unfolding.

A clear update can stabilize a situation before the outcome is visible. A vague or delayed update can create enough uncertainty to change how others use you, how quickly decisions move, and how much oversight gathers around the problem.

Communication as a Signal

Every communication does double work.

It carries information about the situation, but it also signals what kind of leader you are while the situation is still moving. People are not only listening for status. They are listening for control, judgment, honesty, and whether they need to get more involved than they expected.

When your communication is clean, people relax faster because the risk is visible and the work is being managed. When it is vague, late, defensive, or overly polished, they begin protecting themselves from what they cannot see.

That is why communication shapes Brand Worth. It teaches people whether your name reduces uncertainty or creates more of it.

Truth, Tone, and Timing

Strong communication protects trust through three disciplines: truth, tone, and timing.

Truth means the message is accurate enough for others to make decisions with it. It does not hide material risk, soften reality beyond usefulness, or make the situation sound better than it is.

Tone means the message carries enough control that it does not transfer unnecessary pressure to others. Calm does not mean emotionless. It means disciplined enough that the communication helps stabilize the environment.

Timing means the message arrives early enough to matter. Information that comes too late may still be true, but it no longer gives others room to act.

When truth, tone, and timing work together, communication becomes a trust multiplier. When one breaks, uncertainty grows.

Figure 9 shows how the three disciplines work together to give people usable reality while there is still room to act.

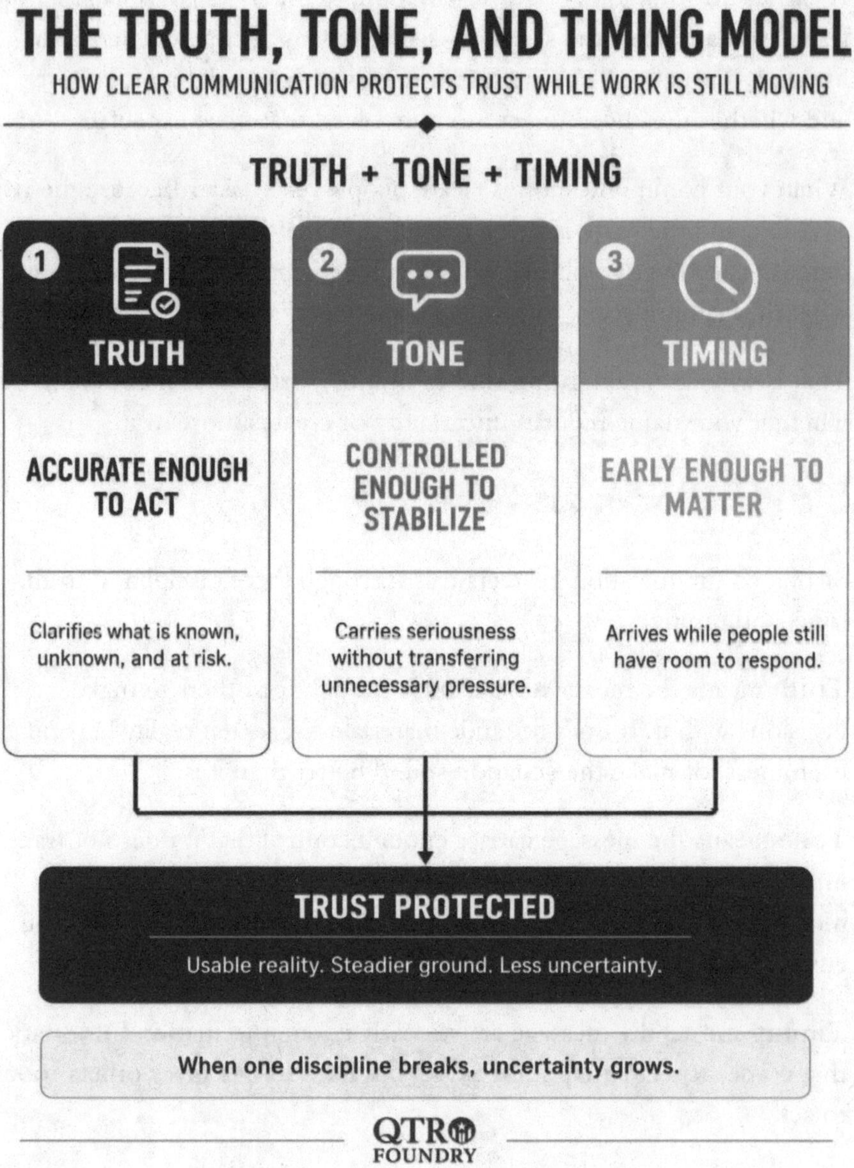

Figure 9 — The Truth, Tone, and Timing Model

Truth, tone, and timing determine the quality of your communication. When all three work together, trust is protected and people can act with confidence.

Truth: Usable Reality

Truth is not simply the absence of lying. In leadership communication, truth means giving people reality they can use.

A technically accurate message can still be unhelpful if it hides the real risk, buries the consequence, or avoids the decision that needs to be made. The question is not only, **"Is this true?"** The question is, **"Is this clear enough for others to act on?"**

Useful truth names what is known, what is unknown, what is at risk, and what happens next. It does not dramatize. It does not conceal. It gives people enough reality to plan.

Tone: Controlled Presence

Tone becomes most important when pressure is already in the room.

A sharp update can make a solvable issue feel heavier. A defensive response can turn a question into a conflict. A vague reassurance can make people wonder what is being protected. A controlled tone does not erase the seriousness of the issue. It makes the seriousness easier to carry.

People remember tone because it tells them whether your presence added stability or strain. Tone is not cosmetic. It is operational. It affects whether the room becomes clearer or more reactive after you communicate.

Timing: Before Uncertainty Spreads

Timing determines whether communication protects trust or arrives too late to help.

Many people wait until they have complete information before communicating. The instinct is understandable, but it can be costly.

When people hear nothing, they do not assume nothing is happening. They fill the silence with concern, follow-up, and protection.

Early communication does not require perfect certainty. It requires responsible clarity.

A useful early message can be simple:

"I see the issue. I am confirming scope now. Current risk is timing. I will update you by 3:00 p.m."

That message does not pretend to know everything. It tells people the risk is visible, the response is active, and the next update will come.

The Four-Line Communication Standard

When stakes are high or uncertainty is growing, communication should answer four questions:

- What is happening?
- What does it affect?
- What are we doing now?
- When will the next update come?

A simple structure works:

- **Status:** What is happening.
- **Risk:** What it affects.
- **Action:** What is being done now.
- **Next update:** When people will hear from you again.

This structure is not bureaucracy. It is a way to reduce uncertainty quickly.

Communication Breakdowns

Communication usually breaks in predictable places.

- It breaks when people wait too long because they want better information.
- It breaks when they soften the truth to avoid discomfort.
- It breaks when tone becomes reactive and spreads pressure.
- It breaks when the update explains activity but not consequence.
- It breaks when no one closes the loop and others are left to guess whether the issue is handled.

Each breakdown teaches something. Not always loudly, but clearly enough over time.

If your communication repeatedly arrives late, people learn to chase. If it hides risk, people learn to verify. If it carries tension, people learn to brace. If it closes cleanly, people learn to trust.

Communication and Closure

Truth, tone, and timing determine the quality of the message. Closure determines whether the communication loop is complete.

Closure is one of the most overlooked parts of communication.

Many professionals give updates while work is active, then disappear at the finish line. They assume completion speaks for itself. It rarely does.

A clean close makes three things visible to the right people:

- The requirement was met.
- Acceptance was confirmed.

- The next step is clear.

Without that visibility, the work may be complete, but the communication loop remains open.

A simple close can sound like this:

"Complete. Requirement met. Acceptance confirmed. Next step is..."

That final sentence protects Brand Worth by preventing others from having to chase clarity after the work is done.

Communication Under Pressure

Pressure does not excuse poor communication. It makes communication more important.

When pressure rises, the room needs fewer dramatic explanations and more usable clarity: what happened, what it affects, what is being done, and when people will hear more.

Communication that provides those answers reduces the burden others have to carry. Silence, over-explanation, softened truth, or reactive tone makes the moment harder than it already is.

7-Day Communication Audit

For the next seven days, examine your communication through three questions:

- Did I tell the truth clearly enough for others to act?
- Did my tone create control or add strain?
- Did my timing give people room to respond?

Then look for the pattern.

Where do you most often lose Brand Worth through communication? Do you wait too long? Soften the truth? Over-explain? Sound sharper than you intended? Leave closure implied?

The point is not to judge your intent. It is to see what your communication is teaching others to expect from your name.

Workbook Link

Complete **Section VII — Communication Audit** using three messages: one routine, one difficult, and one involving incomplete information. Examine where truth, tone, and timing protected trust—and whether you closed the communication loop visibly.

The Standard

Communication should make your leadership easier to trust while the work is still moving.

Communication protects trust when the truth is clear, the tone is controlled, the timing is early enough to matter, and the loop closes visibly.

Your name gains value when your communication gives others usable reality, steadier ground, and less uncertainty than they had before.

Part IV — Scaling Brand Worth

Brand Worth does not end with personal reputation.

At its highest level, the value attached to your name begins to affect other people. It shapes who you develop, who you recommend, who gains access through your judgment, and what standards continue moving when you are not in the room.

That is the work of Part IV.

The first three parts of this book focused on what your name carries, how it is built, and how it is protected under pressure. Part IV asks a larger question: **What does your name make possible for others?**

Mentorship transfers your standard. Sponsorship places your name behind someone else's opportunity. Legacy is the value that continues after your direct presence, title, or authority is gone.

These are not sentimental ideas. They are practical extensions of Brand Worth. A name with real weight can open doors for others, but only when that weight has been earned through trust, consistency, and delivered results.

Part IV is about stewarding Brand Worth responsibly.

The chapters that follow show how your name can develop people, extend opportunity, and leave behind standards others can carry.

Figure 10 — The Brand Worth Scaling Model

How Brand Worth extends beyond individual performance by transferring standards through mentorship, extending responsible opportunity through sponsorship, and compounding into legacy.

Part IV — The Standard

Brand Worth scales when your name creates value beyond your own performance. It transfers through mentorship, extends through sponsorship, and compounds into legacy when the standard attached to your name continues to help others after your direct presence is gone.

Chapter 10 — Mentorship: Brand Transfer

Your Brand Worth shapes more than how people experience you. It also shapes what others learn from being close to you.

Every leader transfers something. Sometimes it is discipline. Sometimes it is urgency without clarity. Sometimes it is calm under pressure. Sometimes it is silence, avoidance, or inconsistency. Whether intentional or not, the people around you are learning what your standard looks like in motion.

That is why mentorship matters to Brand Worth.

Mentorship is not merely advice, encouragement, or career guidance. At its strongest, mentorship is **Brand Transfer:** the movement of your standard into someone else's judgment, behavior, and work.

The question is not only, **"Who am I helping?"**

The deeper question is, **"What standard am I transferring?"**

What Mentorship Actually Transfers

People do not learn leadership primarily through instruction. They learn it through observation. They watch what you do when conditions are difficult, how you communicate when risk appears, whether your tone stays controlled, whether you own mistakes, whether your standard changes under pressure, and whether you close loops when the work is uncomfortable.

Over time, they begin to mirror the pattern—not perfectly, but consistently enough that your influence becomes visible in their behavior.

The Echo of the Standard

Maria was a Senior Director of Operations whose name meant one thing to the executive team: no surprises. If risk appeared, she surfaced it early. If a deadline moved, she communicated before people had to ask. If something broke, she owned the response and gave the organization a path forward.

When Ben was promoted into his first project manager role, Maria did more than teach him systems, templates, and company procedures. She taught him her standard.

When he found a minor error, she made him report it immediately. When he prepared status updates, she pushed him to be clearer. When he wanted to wait for more information before communicating a possible delay, she corrected him.

Over time, Ben stopped merely hearing the standard and began carrying it.

The test came while Maria was on vacation. A Tier 1 supplier abruptly halted operations, threatening Ben's largest Q3 project. His first instinct was panic. He wanted to wait, gather more information, and hope the issue stabilized before it became visible.

But the standard Maria had taught him was already doing its work.

Ben surfaced the issue immediately, named the risk, brought two alternative suppliers his team was already vetting, and gave a clear next-update time.

When Maria returned, the VP of Operations stopped her before she could apologize for the disruption.

"Don't worry about it," he said. **"Ben handled it exactly the way you would have."**

That was the moment Maria knew the transfer had worked. She had not only developed an employee. She had built someone who could carry her standard when she was not present.

What Maria Transferred

Maria did not transfer personality. She transferred discipline.

Ben did not succeed because he copied her style. He succeeded because he had absorbed her operating standard: surface risk early, communicate clearly, own the response, bring options, and close uncertainty before it spreads.

That is Brand Transfer. A mentor's standard becomes visible in someone else's behavior.

Why This Matters

Every leader creates influence. Not every leader scales it.

Influence tied only to your presence has a limit. Mentorship allows your standard to operate through another person. That is how Brand Worth begins to multiply.

Multiplication or Dilution

Mentorship creates one of two outcomes: **multiplication** or **dilution.**

Multiplication happens when people carry your standard accurately. They communicate the way you taught them, make decisions through the principles you reinforced, and handle pressure with the discipline you modeled.

Dilution happens when the standard becomes unclear. People imitate pieces of your approach but miss the judgment behind it. They repeat your language without carrying your discipline.

That weakens Brand Worth because the people associated with you begin producing uneven outcomes.

Mentorship Is Not Casual

Effective mentorship is structured, not stiff.

It requires clear expectations, direct feedback, modeled behavior, repeated correction, and a standard the other person can actually apply.

Encouragement matters, but encouragement without a standard creates risk. If you do not define the standard early, you will spend the relationship correcting drift later.

The mentor's job is not only to help someone feel more confident. It is to make the standard visible enough that confidence has something reliable to stand on.

The Standard You Carry

People do not adopt what you say once. They adopt what you demonstrate repeatedly.

If your behavior is inconsistent, they learn inconsistency. If your standards shift under pressure, they learn that standards are conditional. If your communication goes silent when things get difficult, they learn silence. If your discipline holds, they learn discipline.

Your example is not background noise. In mentorship, it becomes curriculum.

The Scaling Point

Every leader reaches a limit. You cannot be in every meeting, make every decision, or personally protect every standard.

But you can build people who carry the standard forward.

Leadership begins to scale when the people you develop can make aligned decisions without waiting for you to approve every move. They know what matters, what good looks like, what is unacceptable, when to communicate, and how to close the loop.

Your presence is no longer required for your standard to operate.

The Mentorship Session Model

A useful mentorship conversation can follow four moves:

Situation → Standard → Options → Commitment

Situation means starting with the actual issue rather than vague advice.

Standard means naming what right looks like and what must be protected.

Options means working through the available paths and the risks each one carries.

Commitment means ending with a clear action: what will be done, by when, who needs to know, and when closure will be visible.

Without that final step, mentorship becomes reflection without transfer.

The Risk of Neglecting Mentorship

If you do not mentor intentionally, your standard still transfers—but often poorly.

People fill in gaps, imitate the loudest behavior, and treat what you tolerate as what you value. That creates drift. Drift becomes inconsistency, not because people lack ability, but because the standard was never made clear enough to carry.

A leader who neglects mentorship leaves the standard to chance, and chance is a poor scaling strategy.

The Operating Shift

Once you understand mentorship as Brand Transfer, your question changes.

You stop asking only, **"How do I help this person grow?"** and begin asking, **"What standard am I transferring?"**

That shift forces you to clarify what should be repeated, corrected, protected, and carried forward.

The quality of your mentorship is not measured by how much advice you give. It is measured by what another person can carry well without you.

Workbook Link

Complete **Section IX — Mentorship & Sponsorship**. Identify the standard you most want the next leader you develop to carry, then use the three **Situation → Standard → Options → Commitment** conversations to test whether that standard is becoming visible in practice.

The Standard

If your influence depends entirely on your presence, it will not scale.

Mentorship should not end with advice that disappears after the conversation, expectations that weaken in your absence, or development without a standard the other person can carry.

Your standard should move through other people clearly enough that the work still reflects it when you are not there to reinforce it yourself.

Chapter 11 — Sponsorship: Risk Extension

Mentorship develops people. Sponsorship places your name behind their next level of access.

Mentorship often happens in private. Sponsorship happens in rooms where decisions carry consequence. It is the moment your judgment becomes part of someone else's opportunity.

That is why sponsorship matters so much to Brand Worth. When you put your name behind someone, your credibility does not stand beside the decision; it enters it.

If the person performs well, your judgment is validated. If they create avoidable risk, your judgment is questioned.

Sponsorship is not casual support. It is risk extension.

An Endorsement Under Risk

The executive board of a rapidly scaling logistics firm was deadlocked over who should lead a high-risk, multimillion-dollar supply chain integration. The CEO wanted an external consultant. The CFO wanted to assign the work to an overextended senior director.

Victor, the Vice President of Operations, interrupted the debate.

He wanted Priya, a mid-level manager the board barely knew. On paper, she did not have the résumé they expected. But Victor had watched her pattern for two years. He had seen how she surfaced risk, how she communicated under strain, how she closed loops, and how her standard held when the room got harder.

So he said what changed the room:

"I want Priya to lead it."

When the CEO challenged the choice, Victor did not retreat into vague praise. He explained the evidence. Then he made the line explicit:

"She is ready, and she is safe with my name. If she fails, hold me accountable for the recommendation."

The board approved the decision because Victor's name already carried judgment they trusted. Over the next eight months, Priya led the integration cleanly. Her performance raised her own Brand Worth, but it also strengthened Victor's. His endorsement had been proven sound.

That is what disciplined sponsorship does: it creates access for the person being sponsored and strengthens the sponsor's credibility when the judgment proves sound.

What Victor Actually Did

Victor did three disciplined things.

He judged readiness through behavior, not hope. He made the endorsement public in the room where the decision carried consequence. And he accepted accountability for the recommendation instead of offering soft praise from a safe distance.

That is what made the sponsorship credible. He was not only saying Priya had potential. He was saying her pattern had earned the opportunity and justified the risk.

What Sponsorship Really Is

Sponsorship is often confused with mentorship, encouragement, or informal support. None of those, by itself, is sponsorship.

Sponsorship moves a person into a room, role, project, or opportunity they may not have reached on their own, and it does so with your name attached.

That is why sponsorship is not generosity without discipline. It is an act of judgment.

The Weight of Your Name

When your name carries Brand Worth, it can reduce hesitation for someone else. People may not know the person you are sponsoring well enough to judge readiness independently, but they know what your name usually means.

They know whether your endorsements hold. They know whether your judgment has been reliable.

That is what makes sponsorship powerful and dangerous at the same time. Once your name is attached, the outcome no longer belongs only to the other person. It reflects back on you.

The Core Question

Every sponsorship decision eventually narrows to one question:

Is this person safe with my name?

Not because you like them. Not because they deserve encouragement. Not because they have potential in the abstract.

Safe with my name does not mean familiar, agreeable, or similar to me. It means the person's demonstrated pattern provides evidence of judgment, reliability, clean communication, coachability, discretion, and follow-through.

The question is whether their pattern is disciplined enough to make your endorsement responsible. Have they held the standard, surfaced risk early, protected trust under pressure, and closed loops cleanly enough to confirm your judgment once the room says yes?

Why Sponsorship Is Rare

Sponsorship is rare not because opportunity is scarce, but because disciplined trust is scarce.

Many leaders will advise someone. Fewer will place their name behind a person in a room where the decision carries real consequence because sponsorship exposes the sponsor's judgment. If the person succeeds, that judgment gains weight. If the person creates avoidable risk, it loses weight.

Evidence should come before endorsement. Hope is not a sponsorship strategy.

Capability and Trustworthiness

Many capable people are not yet ready for sponsorship.

Capability answers whether someone can do the work. Sponsorship asks a harder question: will they do it consistently, cleanly, and without creating unnecessary risk?

A talented person who still needs constant follow-up, hides risk, becomes defensive under correction, or mishandles sensitive context may be capable and still not be safe with your name.

Sponsorship is based less on the best version of someone than on the version likely to appear when pressure increases.

What Readiness Looks Like

Readiness for sponsorship usually reveals itself through a small set of repeated signals:

- **Reliability:** They keep commitments or renegotiate early.
- **Clean communication:** They surface risk before others have to ask.
- **Visible closure:** They make completion clear instead of leaving uncertainty behind.
- **Coachability:** They take correction without turning it into a contest.
- **Discretion:** They can carry trust and sensitive context without leaking either.

If one of these signals remains unproven, sponsorship requires more testing before the recommendation becomes responsible.

How Sponsorship Decisions Are Made

Responsible sponsors rarely leap from admiration to endorsement.

They observe someone over time, test readiness through smaller responsibilities, watch how the person communicates under pressure, and look for whether the standard holds when the work becomes more exposed.

The room may hear only one sentence—"You can trust them"—but behind it should be repeated evidence, not vague enthusiasm.

Asking for Sponsorship

If you want sponsorship, start by becoming safe with someone's name.

Give them evidence: keep your commitments, communicate before they have to chase you, surface risk early, take correction without defensiveness, protect sensitive context, and close loops cleanly.

Then make the ask specific.

Not **"Can you sponsor me?"** but:

"What would you need to see from me before you would be comfortable putting your name behind me for broader work?"

That question shows maturity because it asks for a standard, not a favor.

The Cost of a Bad Bet

Poor sponsorship decisions cost more than a single failed opportunity. They weaken the sponsor's future endorsements, increase skepticism in the room, and make later recommendations harder to advance.

That does not mean every sponsored person must perform perfectly. No leader controls every outcome. But there is a difference between a reasonable risk and an undisciplined bet.

A reasonable risk is based on observed pattern. An undisciplined bet is based on preference, politics, guilt, friendship, pressure, or hope.

Sponsorship without evidence is generosity that outruns judgment.

Sponsorship as a System

At scale, sponsorship should not depend only on personal preference or informal access. Healthy organizations establish clearer readiness standards so opportunity does not flow only to the most visible, familiar, or politically connected people.

That does not remove judgment. It disciplines judgment.

A strong sponsorship system asks:

- What evidence shows this person is ready?
- What risk would this opportunity expose?
- What support or guardrails would help them succeed?

- Who is willing to put their name behind the recommendation?
- What would confirm that the endorsement was sound?

When sponsorship becomes disciplined, it expands opportunity without lowering standards.

Workbook Link

Complete **Part II** of **Section IX — Mentorship & Sponsorship** and assess one person you may be preparing to sponsor. Identify the evidence already established, the readiness signal still unproven, and the next assignment that would make the decision responsible.

The Standard

Your name should create opportunity for others without creating unnecessary risk.

Sponsorship should never become endorsement without evidence, access without standards, or generosity that outruns judgment. Disciplined sponsorship expands opportunity while protecting the credibility behind the endorsement.

If your name opens the door, their pattern must be ready to walk through it.

Chapter 12 — Legacy: Your Name as an Asset

Legacy is not what people say about you at the end. It is what continues to function because of how you led.

That distinction matters because many leaders think about legacy too late. They wait until a transition, retirement, promotion, or departure before asking what their leadership will leave behind. By then, much of the answer has already been written.

Legacy is built earlier. It is built in the standards you protect, the people you develop, the decisions you shape, the trust you preserve, and the systems that become stronger because your name was attached to them.

A strong name does more than open doors while you are present. Over time, it becomes an asset others can still use after you leave the room.

What Legacy Really Measures

Legacy measures continuation.

- What still works when you are not there?
- What standards still hold without your direct supervision?
- Who makes better decisions because of what they learned from you?
- What trust remains attached to your name after the title changes, the role ends, or the room moves on?

Those questions keep legacy from becoming sentiment. They turn it into evidence.

A Real Example: What Remains

Robert had led a regional operations division for seven years. He was respected, but not because he tried to be the center of every decision. His strength was different. He built standards people could use without waiting for him.

He required early risk communication. He expected clean handoffs. He made leaders own misses without drama and fix the system behind them. He promoted people who could carry judgment, not just people who performed well when watched.

When Robert accepted a national role, his departure created concern. The region had grown under his leadership, and several executives wondered whether performance would drop once he was no longer present.

It did not.

His successor, Tanya, had been developed within the standards Robert protected. She did not copy his personality, but she carried the discipline. The weekly operating rhythm continued. Risk updates came early. Managers closed loops visibly. Failure reviews remained direct but constructive. Within six months, the region was performing at the same level and developing leaders even faster.

Robert's legacy was not that people missed him. They did. But the deeper evidence was that the system still worked.

His name had become an asset because the standard attached to it survived his absence.

Legacy Is Built Through Transfer

Legacy is not built by being indispensable. It is built by making the right things repeatable.

If everything depends on your presence, your influence may be strong, but it is not yet durable. People may admire you, rely on you, and perform well around you. The test is what happens when your direct involvement decreases.

- Do decisions stay aligned?
- Do standards hold?
- Do people communicate risk early?
- Do they recover cleanly from misses?
- Do they develop others with the same discipline?

If the answer is yes, your Brand Worth has moved beyond personal reputation. It is operating through other people.

The Asset Value of a Name

A name becomes an asset when it carries usable confidence beyond the person who owns it.

Inside an organization, certain names begin to mean something stable. A name can mean judgment. It can mean calm under pressure. It can mean clean execution, no surprises, principled decisions, or leaders who develop other leaders.

That kind of name has value because it reduces uncertainty. People know what standard is likely to follow when the name is attached to a project, recommendation, hire, or decision.

The asset value of a name is never automatic. It is built through accumulated evidence and protected through disciplined behavior. It appreciates through trust, consistency, and delivered results. It depreciates through neglect, ego, avoidance, and standards that weaken when no one is watching.

The Three Components of Legacy

Legacy becomes durable through three connected elements:

Integrity → Impact → Investment

Integrity is the standard your name remains trusted for.
Impact is the value your work continues to create.
Investment is the people and systems prepared to carry that value forward.

Integrity gives legacy credibility. Impact gives it consequence. Investment gives it continuity.

What You Leave in People

The most durable part of legacy often lives in people.

People carry the standards they learned from you into rooms you will never enter. They repeat your language, your expectations, your tolerances, and your way of handling pressure. They also repeat what you allowed.

That is why legacy is not only about what you taught intentionally. It is also about what your behavior made normal.

If you tolerated vague commitments, people learned that vagueness was acceptable. If you allowed silence under pressure, people learned that silence could pass. If you corrected drift, named standards clearly, and modeled ownership, people learned that too.

Legacy travels through what people believe is normal because of you.

What You Leave in Systems

Legacy also lives in systems.

A system can be a meeting rhythm, a decision standard, a handoff practice, a recovery protocol, a communication cadence, or a way of developing leaders. If the system makes better behavior easier after you leave, it becomes part of your legacy.

Personality does not scale as well as structure. A charismatic leader may create energy while present, but if that energy depends entirely on their presence, it fades when they leave. A disciplined leader builds systems that keep producing clarity after the room changes.

The Danger of Being Indispensable

Many leaders mistake indispensability for impact.

They become the person everyone needs, the one who approves every move, solves every issue, and holds every standard personally. That may feel valuable for a season, but it creates dependency.

Dependency is not legacy. It is unfinished transfer.

If people cannot make aligned decisions without you, your leadership has not yet become durable. If standards weaken in your absence, they were attached too tightly to you and not clearly enough to the system.

The strongest leaders do not build dependence on themselves. They build capacity that continues without constant access to them.

Stewardship of Brand Worth

At this stage, Brand Worth becomes stewardship.

You are no longer asking only, **"What does my name open for me?"** You are asking, **"What does my name make stronger beyond me?"**

That question changes how you lead. It makes development more intentional, sponsorship more disciplined, systems more important, and standards more visible.

Stewardship means protecting the value attached to your name so it can create value for others without losing integrity.

The Legacy Check

If you want to test the legacy your name is building, ask five questions:

- What standard would people associate with my name without needing explanation?
- Who is better prepared to lead because they worked with me?
- What decision, process, or rhythm is stronger because I protected it?
- Where does my influence still depend too heavily on my personal presence?
- What would weaken if I left tomorrow?

Those questions reveal whether your Brand Worth is becoming durable or merely visible.

Workbook Link

Complete **Section X — Legacy Check**. Use **Integrity → Impact → Investment** to examine what your name is leaving in people, systems, and standards—and whether that value can continue without your direct presence.

The Standard

Legacy should leave something useful behind.

Legacy is not admiration without transfer, dependence without capacity, or a name people praise but cannot build from.

Your name becomes an asset—and Brand Worth becomes legacy—when the standards attached to it continue creating clarity, trust, and disciplined action without your direct presence.

WORKBOOK — THE BRAND WORTH SYSTEM

This workbook is the operating layer of the book. The chapters explain the Brand Worth System; these pages help you run it against your own behavior.

Brand Worth is not built by understanding the system alone. It is built by applying the system in real situations until your behavior becomes new evidence.

Use this workbook to diagnose what your name currently carries, identify where trust is leaking, and choose the correction most likely to make your name easier to choose, trust, and build around over time.

How to Use This Workbook

Work through one section at a time. Diagnose the current pattern, identify the behavior creating it, and choose one correction. Use each section's exercise to examine that pattern in real situations. Then carry one priority correction into **Section VIII — Consistency Tracker** and test it for seven days.

The goal is not to judge your intent. It is to inspect your pattern clearly enough to change it. After the seven-day test, use the **Final Commitment** to turn the most consequential correction into 30 days of repeated evidence.

Developmental Use: The scoring tools in this workbook are reflection and development aids, not validated psychological, clinical, or employment assessments. Use them to identify patterns and priorities, not as the sole basis for personnel decisions.

The workbook moves the system from understanding into practice through a simple operating cycle: diagnose the current pattern, choose one correction, apply it in real situations, and review the evidence. Figure 11 shows that cycle at a glance.

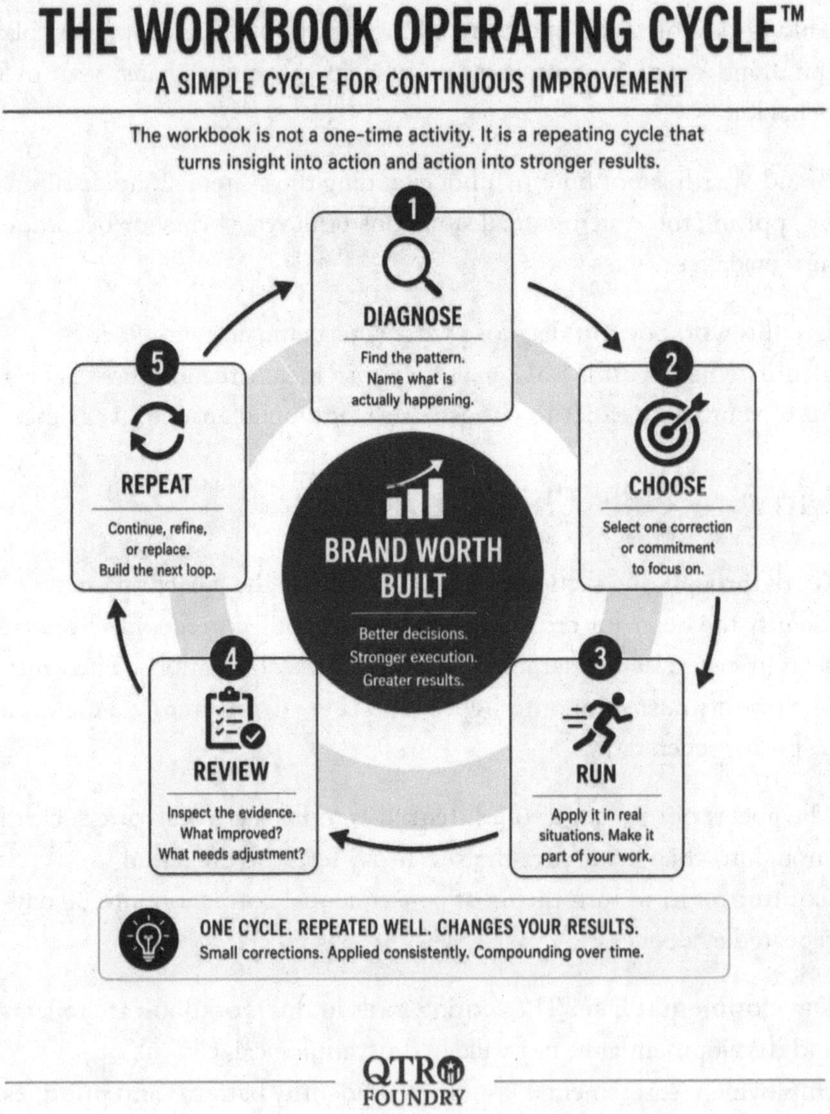

Figure 11 — The Workbook Operating Cycle

How deliberate behavior becomes repeated evidence.

Workbook Quick Reference

Use this guide to find the workbook tools referenced throughout the book. Each section turns one part of Brand Worth into something you can diagnose, test, and strengthen through action.

Section I — The Name Test

Diagnose what your name currently triggers in decision-making environments and identify one priority correction.

Section II — Define Your Brand Worth

Define the observable standard, behavior, evidence, and signal you want your name to carry.

Section III — The Brand Worth Equation

Score Trust, Consistency, and Delivered Results, then identify the multiplier and behavior currently limiting your Brand Worth.

Section IV — The Reliability Loop

Run one active commitment through clarity, commitment, cadence, and closure to identify where reliability is most likely to break.

Section V — Pressure Response

Test whether your response creates control or transfers volatility across three meaningful pressure events.

Section VI — Failure Response

Apply the Recovery Protocol to one meaningful failure and two additional recovery events.

Section VII — Communication Audit

Examine one routine, one difficult, and one incomplete-information message through truth, tone, and timing—and visible closure.

Section VIII — Consistency Tracker

Test whether your commitments, communication, pressure response, and closure remain dependable while you practice one priority correction for seven days.

Section IX — Mentorship & Sponsorship

Test whether your standard is transferring through another person and whether that person's demonstrated pattern is ready for your name.

Section X — Legacy Check

Test whether your standards, impact, and investment in people and systems can continue without your direct presence.

Final Commitment

Turn the workbook's most consequential insight into 30 days of repeated evidence.

SECTION I — THE NAME TEST

Primary Diagnostic

When your name is mentioned in a room you are not in, what happens most often?

Choose the most honest answer.

1. Avoidance

People say:

"Let's go another direction."
"Not for this one."
"Choose someone safer."

You are bypassed because your name carries too much risk for the moment.

2. Hesitation

People say:

"I'm not sure."
"Can they handle this?"
"Do we have another option?"

The room slows down because your name creates concern.

3. Validation

People say:

"Let me confirm."
"Check with someone first."
"Make sure we have backup."

Work pauses because your name still requires verification.

4. Acceleration

People say:

"Put them on it."
"They've got it."
"Ask them."

Work moves forward because your name reduces uncertainty.

5. Decision Pull

People say:

"Let's get them involved."
"Bring them in."
"I want their input."

Your name becomes a reason to move forward because others expect your involvement to improve the outcome.

Your Current State

Circle one:

Avoidance / Hesitation / Validation / Acceleration / Decision Pull

Evidence

Write three recent moments that support this assessment.

Pattern Check

What behavior most likely created this current state? Circle any that apply.

- Missed commitments
- Late communication
- Strong delivery
- Clean closure
- Inconsistent follow-through
- Stable pressure response
- Unclear ownership
- Reliable judgment
- Other: ______________________________

The Question That Matters

What does your name currently make easier?

What does your name currently make harder?

One Priority Correction

Choose one behavior that would strengthen or protect what your name currently triggers.

My priority correction:

The current behavior it will replace:

The trigger that should remind me to use it:

The signal I want this correction to create:

I will carry this correction into **Section VIII — Consistency Tracker** if it remains the highest-priority correction after I complete **Sections II–VII**.

SECTION II — DEFINE YOUR BRAND WORTH

Your Brand Worth Statement

Complete this sentence:

My name will stand for:

Keep it specific.

A useful Brand Worth statement is:

- behavior-based
- measurable
- observable
- repeatable

A weak statement sounds impressive but cannot be tested.

A strong statement tells people what they can expect from you.

Clarity Test

Read your statement and answer:

Can someone observe this behavior?

Yes / No

Can someone measure whether I did it?

Yes / No

Can I repeat it under pressure?

Yes / No

Would this reduce uncertainty for others?

Yes / No

If the answer is **"No"** to any of these, rewrite the statement.

Operating Behavior

What is one behavior I will use consistently to make this statement real?

____

When and where should this behavior appear?

____

What evidence would show that it is becoming dependable?

____

Non-Negotiable Standard

What will I not compromise, even under pressure?

____

Under what condition is this standard hardest to hold?

What will I do when that condition appears?

Signal You Want to Create

When my name comes up, what should people immediately associate with it?

Examples:

- clean communication
- no surprises
- disciplined follow-through
- calm under pressure
- trusted judgment
- clean delivery
- ownership without excuses

My intended signal:

What should people experience differently when this signal becomes believable?

Evidence Required

What evidence would prove that my name is starting to carry this signal?

Who is most likely to experience that evidence?

Priority Action

The behavior I will prioritize to reinforce this signal:

The trigger that should remind me to use it:

The current behavior it will replace:

I will carry this behavior into **Section VIII — Consistency Tracker** if it remains the highest-priority correction after I complete **Sections III–VII.**

SECTION III — THE BRAND WORTH EQUATION

Brand Worth = Trust × Consistency × Delivered Results

Score each multiplier honestly. Because the equation is multiplicative, weakness in one area lowers the strength of the whole system. Trust without consistency becomes fragile. Consistency without delivered results becomes activity. Delivered results without trust create risk.

Use the same scoring standard for all three multipliers:

1 — Repeatedly creates uncertainty
3 — Inconsistent or dependent on conditions
5 — Dependable, even when conditions change

Use 2 or 4 when the evidence falls between those anchors. Do not average the scores. The purpose is to identify the multiplier most limiting your Brand Worth.

Trust

Do people believe your word when others are depending on you and conditions change?

Circle one:

1 / 2 / 3 / 4 / 5

Evidence supporting this score:

What behavior currently weakens trust?

Consistency

Does your standard hold across pressure, complexity, and competing priorities?

Circle one:

1 / 2 / 3 / 4 / 5

Evidence supporting this score:

Where does your consistency break most often?

Delivered Results

Do you finish cleanly, close loops, and move outcomes forward without constant supervision?

Circle one:

1 / 2 / 3 / 4 / 5

Evidence supporting this score:

Where do your results lose value?

Multiplier Assessment

Strongest multiplier:

____

Weakest multiplier:

____

The multiplier currently limiting my Brand Worth:

____

The behavior creating that limitation:

____

The first correction I will test:

____

Trust Deposit Discipline

Review the last seven days. Mark whether your behavior made each of these four trust deposits.

Did I make fewer commitments and keep them?

Yes / No

Did I renegotiate early when something was at risk?

Yes / No

Did I close visibly with "Complete + next step"?

Yes / No

Did I own the break cleanly when something went wrong?

Yes / No

The trust deposit I made most consistently:

The deposit I missed most often:

My correction:

Clean Finish Standard

Choose one recently completed assignment.

Assignment:

Was the requirement met?

Yes / No

Was acceptance confirmed?

Yes / No

Was the next step stated?

Yes / No

If one of these is missing, the work may be complete, but the uncertainty is not.

What will I do to close it?

Pricing Signal Audit

Review three recent requests, interactions, or commitments. The goal is not to judge isolated moments. It is to see what your repeated signals are teaching others to expect.

Interaction 1

Situation or commitment:

Did I acknowledge it with a next update time?
Yes / No

Did I communicate risk before the deadline?
Yes / No / Not applicable

Did I close the loop visibly with "Complete + next step"?
Yes / No

What did this interaction teach others to expect?

Interaction 2

Situation or commitment:

Did I acknowledge it with a next update time?
Yes / No

Did I communicate risk before the deadline?
Yes / No / Not applicable

Did I close the loop visibly with "Complete + next step"?
Yes / No

What did this interaction teach others to expect?

Interaction 3

Situation or commitment:

Did I acknowledge it with a next update time?
Yes / No

Did I communicate risk before the deadline?
Yes / No / Not applicable

Did I close the loop visibly with "Complete + next step"?
Yes / No

What did this interaction teach others to expect?

Pricing Review

Which signal did I reinforce most consistently?

Where did my Brand Worth leak?

What behavior caused the leak?

The correction I will carry into **Section VIII — Consistency Tracker**:

The signal I want that correction to create:

SECTION IV — THE RELIABILITY LOOP

Reliability is not a personality trait. It is a loop: **clarity, commitment, cadence, and closure.** When reliability breaks, it usually breaks in one of those four places.

Use this section to run one active commitment through the complete loop, identify where reliability is most likely to break, and close the work without leaving others to guess.

Choose One Active Commitment

Project, task, or responsibility:

____

Who is depending on this?

____

What outcome is expected?

____

Current deadline:

____

Current status:

____

Reliability Loop Scoring

Use the same standard for each part of the loop:

1 — Missing, unclear, or creating uncertainty
3 — Partially defined or inconsistently applied
5 — Clear, visible, and dependable

Use 2 or 4 when the evidence falls between those anchors.

1. Clarity

Before you commit, define what "done" means.

What does done mean?

Who approves or accepts the work?

What standard must be met?

What would make this incomplete?

What is unclear right now?

Clarity Score

Circle one:

1 / 2 / 3 / 4 / 5

What would raise this score by one point?

2. Commitment

A commitment should be precise enough for others to build around.

Strong Commitment:

"I'll send the draft by Thursday at 3:00 p.m."

My exact commitment:

By when:

To whom:

What condition could put this commitment at risk?

If risk appears, by when will I renegotiate?

____

Commitment Score

Circle one:

1 / 2 / 3 / 4 / 5

What would make this commitment cleaner?

____

3. Cadence

Cadence prevents people from guessing.

When will I provide the next update?

____

Who needs to receive it?

____

What should the update include?

____

Use this structure:

Status: ______________________________

Risk: ________________________________

Next step: ______________________________

Next update: ____________________________

Cadence Score

Circle one:

1 / 2 / 3 / 4 / 5

What could cause cadence to break on this commitment?

____

4. Closure

Work is not closed until the right people know three things:

1. The requirement was met.
2. Acceptance was confirmed.
3. The next step is clear.

Use this closure language:

"Complete. Requirement met. Acceptance confirmed. Next step is…"

Draft closure message:

____

Who needs to receive it?

____

What next step must be stated?

Closure Score

Circle one:

1 / 2 / 3 / 4 / 5

What must happen before this loop can close?

Reliability Break Point

Where is reliability most likely to break in this commitment?

Circle one:

Clarity / Commitment / Cadence / Closure

What behavior or condition could cause the break?

What does that break make people wonder?

What correction will I apply to this commitment?

What signal should that correction create?

Complete the Loop

The next action I will take:

By when:

Who needs to know:

My next update will be:

If conditions change, I will renegotiate by:

The closure message I expect to send:

Reliability Review

Complete this review after the commitment closes.

Was “done” clear from the beginning?
Yes / No

Was my commitment precise enough for others to plan around?
Yes / No

Did I communicate before others had to ask?
Yes / No / Not applicable

Did I renegotiate early when conditions changed?
Yes / No / Not applicable

Was acceptance confirmed and the next step made visible?
Yes / No

Which part of the loop held strongest?

____

Which part still broke?

____

What did my behavior teach others to expect?

____

The behavior I will repeat:

____

The correction I will carry into **Section VIII — Consistency Tracker**:

SECTION V — PRESSURE RESPONSE

Pressure does not create your pattern. It reveals it.

Use this section to inspect how you respond when time compresses, stakes rise, and uncertainty increases. The goal is not to judge the moment after the fact. It is to see whether your response creates control or transfers volatility to others.

The Pressure Pattern

What usually happens to me first under pressure?

____

Circle one:

Speed up / Go silent / Over-explain / Get reactive / Overcontrol / Avoid the issue / Stay clear and steady

What does that pattern create for others?

____

Does my pressure response usually create:

Control / Volatility

What evidence supports that answer?

____

The Pressure Response Model

Use this sequence when pressure rises:

Pause → Clarify → Prioritize → Communicate

Pause

Did I control my first reaction before it became someone else's problem?

____

Clarify

Did I identify what mattered most, what was known, what was unknown, and what risk was active?

____

Prioritize

Did I decide what had to happen first, what could wait, and what should stop?

____

Communicate

Did I reduce uncertainty before others had to ask?

____

Current Pressure Event

Describe one recent pressure event that revealed your default pattern:

____

What triggered the pressure?

Circle any that apply:

Time compression / Visibility / High stakes / Unclear information / Competing priorities / Fatigue / Other: __________

What was my first instinct?

____

What did that instinct create for others?

____

Pressure and Control

When pressure rises, where is control most likely to weaken first?

Circle one:

Reaction / Tone / Clarity / Prioritization / Communication / Ownership

What signal does that send?

____

What does that make others do?

____

What should control look like from me under pressure?

____

Pressure Script

Use this when risk is present and others need clarity.

Here is what happened: ________
Here is the risk: ________
Here is what we are doing now: ________
Next update will be at: ________

If you cannot fill in those four lines, pause and clarify before you brief.

Pressure Correction

The pressure behavior I need to interrupt:

The trigger that usually activates it:

The replacement behavior I will use:

The cue that will remind me to pause:

The signal I want my response to create:

Pressure Response Log

Use the next three meaningful pressure moments to test your correction. Do not force a daily example. Use moments when time compresses, stakes rise, or uncertainty increases.

The goal is to see whether your replacement behavior creates control consistently enough to become a new pattern.

Pressure Event 1

Situation:

What triggered the pressure?

What was my first instinct?

Did I pause before reacting?
Yes / No

Did I clarify what was known, unknown, and at risk?
Yes / No

Did I prioritize what had to happen first, what could wait, and what should stop?
Yes / No

Did I communicate before others had to chase me?
Yes / No

Did I use the replacement behavior I identified?
Yes / No

Did my response create control or volatility?
Control / Volatility

What did my response create for others?

What will I repeat or change?

Pressure Event 2

Situation:

What triggered the pressure?

What was my first instinct?

Did I pause before reacting?
Yes / No

Did I clarify what was known, unknown, and at risk?
Yes / No

Did I prioritize what had to happen first, what could wait, and what should stop?
Yes / No

Did I communicate before others had to chase me?
Yes / No

Did I use the replacement behavior I identified?
Yes / No

Did my response create control or volatility?
Control / Volatility

What did my response create for others?

____

What will I repeat or change?

____

Pressure Event 3

Situation:

____

What triggered the pressure?

____

What was my first instinct?

____

Did I pause before reacting?
Yes / No

Did I clarify what was known, unknown, and at risk?
Yes / No

Did I prioritize what had to happen first, what could wait, and what should stop?
Yes / No

Did I communicate before others had to chase me?
Yes / No

Did I use the replacement behavior I identified?
Yes / No

Did my response create control or volatility?
Control / Volatility

What did my response create for others?

What will I repeat or change?

Pressure Review

What pattern appeared across the three events?

What trigger produced the most volatility?

What behavior created the most control?

Where did I transfer pressure to others?

Did the replacement behavior work?
Yes / No / Partially

What still caused the pattern to break?

What pressure habit still needs to be interrupted?

Carry Forward

The pressure behavior I will continue interrupting:

The replacement behavior I will carry into **Section VIII — Consistency Tracker**:

The trigger that will remind me to use it:

The signal I want this response to create:

SECTION VI — FAILURE RESPONSE

Failure does not damage Brand Worth by itself.

The greater risk is what your response teaches others after the miss becomes visible.

Use this section to examine one meaningful failure in depth, review two additional recovery moments, and identify whether your response creates control or uncertainty.

The Failure Pattern

When a mistake becomes visible, what is my first instinct?

Circle one:

Delay / Minimize / Explain / Defend / Fix quietly / Own it / Get clear and respond

What does that instinct usually create for others?

Does my response usually create:

Control / Uncertainty

What evidence supports that answer?

The Recovery Protocol

Use this sequence when something breaks:

Own → Diagnose → Fix → Guardrail → Close

Own

Did I take responsibility for leading the response without delay or deflection?

Diagnose

Did I identify what failed, what allowed it to fail, and what part of the standard was missing or weakened?

Fix

Did I remove the active problem completely enough that people no longer had to wonder whether it was handled?

Guardrail

Did I create a visible change that makes recurrence less likely?

Close

Did I confirm resolution, communicate what changed, and state what happens next?

Primary Failure Analysis

Choose one recent failure, miss, or preventable mistake that best reveals your default recovery pattern:

What made it visible?

When did I know, and when did I communicate?

Who was affected?

What was the real impact?

What part of the standard was missing or weakened?

Ownership Check

Did I own the issue clearly?

Yes / No

If not, what did I do instead?

Circle any that apply:

Delayed / Softened the issue / Explained first / Shifted blame / Avoided the conversation / Hoped it would fade

What did that response make others wonder?

____

Write the ownership statement this moment required:

____

Failure Response Script

Use this when an issue becomes visible, even before every answer is known:

This is on me.
Here is what happened: ________
Here is the current impact: ________
Here is what I am confirming now: ________
Here is what we are doing next: ________
Next update will be at: ________

If the full cause is not yet known, do not wait. State what is known, what you are confirming, what happens next, and when the next update will come.

Forgiveness Capital

In this situation, did my prior pattern buy me trust or cost me trust?

Circle one:

Bought trust / Cost trust

What deposits or withdrawals in my prior pattern influenced that?

____

What kind of response did this moment require?

____

After-Action Note

Complete this after the active issue is stabilized. Keep it brief. The purpose is to create ownership, correction, and confidence before memory becomes vague and explanation becomes self-protective.

What happened?

____

What impact did it create?

____

What was the real cause?

____

What did I fix immediately?

____

What guardrail now exists?

____

How will resolution be confirmed?

____

Recovery Event Reviews

Review two additional mistakes, misses, or correction moments. They do not need to be major events. The goal is to see whether your recovery pattern holds across different situations.

Recovery Event 1

Situation:

What became visible?

Did I own the issue clearly?
Yes / No

Did I diagnose the real cause?
Yes / No

Did I correct the active problem?
Yes / No

Did I create or reinforce a guardrail?
Yes / No / Not needed

Did I close the loop visibly?
Yes / No

Did my response create control or uncertainty?
Control / Uncertainty

What did others learn from how I responded?

What will I repeat or change?

Recovery Event 2

Situation:

What became visible?

Did I own the issue clearly?
Yes / No

Did I diagnose the real cause?
Yes / No

Did I correct the active problem?
Yes / No

Did I create or reinforce a guardrail?
Yes / No / Not needed

Did I close the loop visibly?
Yes / No

Did my response create control or uncertainty?
Control / Uncertainty

What did others learn from how I responded?

What will I repeat or change?

Failure Review

What response pattern appeared across the primary failure and the two recovery events?

Which Recovery Protocol step was strongest?

Which step did I skip or delay most often?

What created the most uncertainty?

What response created the most stability?

Where did I protect my image before protecting trust?

What did others learn from the way I responded?

Carry Forward

The failure-response behavior I need to interrupt:

The replacement behavior I will practice:

The trigger that will remind me to own the issue early:

The Recovery Protocol step I most often skip or delay:

The signal I want my response to create:

The behavior I will carry into **Section VIII — Consistency Tracker**:

SECTION VII — COMMUNICATION AUDIT

Communication is how your leadership is experienced in real time.

Use this audit to examine the three communication disciplines—**truth, tone, and timing**—and whether you close the communication loop visibly.

Truth, tone, and timing determine the quality of the message. Closure determines whether the communication is complete.

Clean Communication Script

Use this when uncertainty appears and others need usable reality:

Here is where we are: ________
Here is the risk: ________
Here is the plan: ________
Next update will be: ________

If you cannot fill in those four lines, pause and clarify before you brief.

Current Communication Pattern

Where does your communication most often break?

Circle one:

Truth / Tone / Timing / Closure

What usually causes the break?

What does that break make people wonder?

What signal does it send?

Truth

Did I say what was actually happening?

Not what sounded better.
Not what bought more time.
Not what avoided discomfort.
What was actually happening.

Where do I tend to soften the truth?

What truth do I need to say more clearly?

Tone

Did my communication create control or add pressure?

Where does my tone change under pressure?

What does that tone create in others?

What should controlled tone sound like for me?

Timing

Did I communicate early enough for others to act?

Where do I tend to wait too long?

Why do I wait?

What should trigger earlier communication?

Closure

Did I make the next step visible enough that others did not have to guess?

Where do I most often leave the communication loop open?

What simple close should I use more consistently?

Three-Message Communication Audit

Review three actual messages that reveal different parts of your communication pattern. Do not use hypothetical examples.

Choose:

1. One routine communication;
2. One difficult communication;
3. One communication sent while information was incomplete.

The goal is to determine whether truth, tone, and timing protected trust—and whether you closed the communication loop visibly.

Message 1 — Routine Communication

Situation:

Who needed the message?

What decision, action, or commitment depended on it?

Truth

Was the message accurate and clear enough for others to act?
Yes / No

What did I state clearly?

What did I soften, bury, or leave unclear?

Tone

Did my tone create control or add strain?
Control / Strain

What did my tone create in others?

Timing

Did the message arrive while others still had room to act?
Yes / No

Did anyone have to chase me?
Yes / No

Closure

Was the next step or next update visible?
Yes / No

Was the communication loop eventually closed?
Yes / No / Still open

What did this message teach others to expect from me?

What will I repeat or change?

Message 2 — Difficult Communication

Use a message involving bad news, disagreement, correction, missed expectations, elevated risk, or an uncomfortable truth.

Situation:

Who needed the message?

What decision, action, or relationship depended on it?

Truth

Was the message accurate and clear enough for others to act?
Yes / No

What did I state clearly?

What did I soften, bury, or leave unclear?

Tone

Did my tone create control or add strain?
Control / Strain

What did my tone create in others?

Timing

Did the message arrive while others still had room to act?
Yes / No

Did anyone have to chase me?
Yes / No

Closure

Was the next step or next update visible?
Yes / No

Was the communication loop eventually closed?
Yes / No / Still open

What did this message teach others to expect from me?

What will I repeat or change?

Message 3 — Incomplete-Information Communication

Use a message sent while pressure was active and all facts were not yet known.

Situation:

Who needed the message?

What decision or action depended on receiving early visibility?

Truth

Did I clearly distinguish what was known, what was unknown, and what was at risk?
Yes / No

What did I state clearly?

What did I soften, bury, or leave unclear?

Tone

Did my tone create control or add strain?
Control / Strain

What did my tone create in others?

Timing

Did I communicate before complete information was available but early enough for others to act?
Yes / No

Did anyone have to chase me?
Yes / No

Closure

Did I provide a clear next-update time?
Yes / No

Was the communication loop eventually closed?
Yes / No / Still open

What did this message teach others to expect from me?

What will I repeat or change?

Communication Review

Across the three messages, where did my communication reduce uncertainty?

Where did it increase uncertainty?

Which communication discipline was strongest?

Truth / Tone / Timing

Which discipline broke most often?

Truth / Tone / Timing

Where did I leave closure implied instead of visible?

When did others have to chase me?

What pattern did my communication teach others to expect?

What communication behavior must I correct first?

Carry Forward

The communication discipline I most need to strengthen:

Truth / Tone / Timing

The communication behavior I need to interrupt:

The replacement behavior I will practice:

The trigger that should cause me to communicate earlier:

The close I will use more consistently:

The signal I want my communication to create:

The behavior I will carry into **Section VIII — Consistency Tracker:**

SECTION VIII — CONSISTENCY TRACKER

Consistency is the proof over time.

Use this tracker to test whether your standard holds when conditions change. Bring forward one priority correction from the earlier workbook sections, practice it for seven days, and review the evidence without explaining away the misses.

Define the Standard

What standard do I want people to count on from me?

____

What behavior proves that standard?

____

What behavior weakens that standard?

____

Under what conditions is this standard hardest to hold?

____

Choose the Correction

Review the behaviors and corrections you identified in **Sections I–VII**. Choose the one behavior that would most strengthen your Brand Worth if it became dependable.

The section where I identified this correction:

The Name Test / Define Your Brand Worth / Brand Worth Equation / Reliability / Pressure / Failure / Communication

The behavior I need to interrupt:

___

The replacement behavior I will practice:

___

The trigger that should remind me to use it:

___

The signal I want the replacement behavior to create:

___

Four Daily Brand Worth Behaviors

For the next seven days, track these four behaviors:

1. Did I keep my commitments or renegotiate early?

   ___

2. Did I communicate before others had to chase me?

   ___

3. Did my standard hold under pressure?

---

4. Did I close loops visibly with "Complete + next step"?

The goal is not to produce perfect days. It is to make your pattern visible enough to change it.

7-Day Consistency Tracker

Day 1

Did I keep my commitments or renegotiate early?
Yes / No / No commitment today

Did I communicate before others had to chase me?
Yes / No / No opportunity

Did my standard hold under pressure?
Yes / No / No pressure event

Did I close loops visibly with "Complete + next step"?
Yes / No / No loop to close

Did I practice my priority correction when the opportunity appeared?
Yes / No / No opportunity

Evidence:

What did today's behavior teach others to expect?

Day 2

Did I keep my commitments or renegotiate early?
Yes / No / No commitment today

Did I communicate before others had to chase me?
Yes / No / No opportunity

Did my standard hold under pressure?
Yes / No / No pressure event

Did I close loops visibly with "Complete + next step"?
Yes / No / No loop to close

Did I practice my priority correction when the opportunity appeared?
Yes / No / No opportunity

Evidence:

What did today's behavior teach others to expect?

Day 3

Did I keep my commitments or renegotiate early?
Yes / No / No commitment today

Did I communicate before others had to chase me?
Yes / No / No opportunity

Did my standard hold under pressure?
Yes / No / No pressure event

Did I close loops visibly with "Complete + next step"?
Yes / No / No loop to close

Did I practice my priority correction when the opportunity appeared?
Yes / No / No opportunity

Evidence:

What did today's behavior teach others to expect?

Day 4

Did I keep my commitments or renegotiate early?
Yes / No / No commitment today

Did I communicate before others had to chase me?
Yes / No / No opportunity

Did my standard hold under pressure?
Yes / No / No pressure event

Did I close loops visibly with "Complete + next step"?
Yes / No / No loop to close

Did I practice my priority correction when the opportunity appeared?
Yes / No / No opportunity

Evidence:

What did today's behavior teach others to expect?

Day 5

Did I keep my commitments or renegotiate early?
Yes / No / No commitment today

Did I communicate before others had to chase me?
Yes / No / No opportunity

Did my standard hold under pressure?
Yes / No / No pressure event

Did I close loops visibly with "Complete + next step"?
Yes / No / No loop to close

Did I practice my priority correction when the opportunity appeared?
Yes / No / No opportunity

Evidence:

What did today's behavior teach others to expect?

Day 6

Did I keep my commitments or renegotiate early?
Yes / No / No commitment today

Did I communicate before others had to chase me?
Yes / No / No opportunity

Did my standard hold under pressure?
Yes / No / No pressure event

Did I close loops visibly with "Complete + next step"?
Yes / No / No loop to close

Did I practice my priority correction when the opportunity appeared?
Yes / No / No opportunity

Evidence:

___

What did today's behavior teach others to expect?

___

Day 7

Did I keep my commitments or renegotiate early?
Yes / No / No commitment today

Did I communicate before others had to chase me?
Yes / No / No opportunity

Did my standard hold under pressure?
Yes / No / No pressure event

Did I close loops visibly with "Complete + next step"?
Yes / No / No loop to close

Did I practice my priority correction when the opportunity appeared?
Yes / No / No opportunity

Evidence:

____

What did today's behavior teach others to expect?

____

Where Consistency Broke

Circle any pattern that appeared:

Overcommitment / Late communication / Reactive tone / Standard drift / Unclear ownership / Incomplete closure / Poor prioritization / Avoiding correction

Which pattern appeared most often?

____

What condition most often triggered it?

Time pressure / Fatigue / Ambiguity / Competing priorities / Conflict / Avoidance / Incomplete information / Other:

____

What did it cost?

____

What did others have to do because of it?

Seven-Day Consistency Review

Which of the four daily behaviors held most consistently?

Which behavior broke most often?

What condition most often triggered the break?

Did my priority correction work?

Yes / No / Partially / Not sufficiently tested

What evidence supports that answer?

What did people learn they can count on from me?

What did people learn they may need to verify?

What standard held?

What standard drifted?

Where did my behavior reduce uncertainty?

Where did it create more?

Next Cycle Decision

Based on the evidence, I will:

Continue the correction / Refine the correction / Replace the correction

Why:

The behavior I will carry forward:

The adjustment I will make:

The trigger I will watch for:

The signal I want the next seven days to reinforce:

SECTION IX — MENTORSHIP & SPONSORSHIP

Scaling Brand Worth means more than building a strong name for yourself.

It means transferring your standard through mentorship and extending your name responsibly through sponsorship.

Use this section to answer two questions:

What standard am I transferring?
Who, if anyone, is becoming safe with my name?

Part I — Mentorship

The Standard I Am Transferring

What is the one standard I most want the next leader I develop to carry?

What does that standard look like in behavior?

What evidence would show that the standard is becoming visible in the other person's judgment, behavior, or work?

____

What behavior would show drift instead?

____

Mentorship Check

Person I will use for this mentorship review:

____

What are they learning from my example right now?

Circle any that apply:

Clarity / Ownership / Communication / Pressure response / Clean finish / Discipline / Inconsistency / Reactivity / Delay / Avoidance

What am I teaching clearly?

____

What am I teaching unintentionally?

____

Where do I need to make the standard more visible?

____

Mentorship Session Model

Use this sequence across the next three meaningful development conversations:

Situation → Standard → Options → Commitment

Situation

What is the real issue or moment that needs attention?

Standard

What standard applies here?

Options

What are the available responses and risks?

Commitment

What will they do, by when, and how will closure be visible?

Three-Conversation Mentorship Transfer Log

Use the same person across three meaningful development conversations. The goal is not to count conversations. It is to see whether the standard becomes visible enough for the other person to carry without waiting for your direction.

Use the **Situation → Standard → Options → Commitment** model in each conversation.

Mentorship Conversation 1

Situation:

____

What standard applied?

____

How did I make the standard visible?

____

What drift needed to be corrected?

____

What options and risks did we examine?

____

Commitment

What will they do?

____

By when?

____

How will closure be visible?

____

What evidence should appear before the next conversation?

____

What evidence actually appeared?

____

What will I reinforce or correct next?

____

Mentorship Conversation 2

Situation:

____

What standard applied?

____

How did I make the standard visible?

____

What drift needed to be corrected?

____

What options and risks did we examine?

____

Commitment

What will they do?

____

By when?

____

How will closure be visible?

____

What evidence should appear before the next conversation?

____

What evidence actually appeared?

____

What will I reinforce or correct next?

____

Mentorship Conversation 3

Situation:

What standard applied?

How did I make the standard visible?

What drift needed to be corrected?

What options and risks did we examine?

Commitment

What will they do?

By when?

How will closure be visible?

What evidence should appear after this conversation?

____

What evidence actually appeared?

____

What will I reinforce or correct next?

____

Mentorship Transfer Review

What standard became clearer across the three conversations?

____

What behavior showed that the standard was beginning to transfer?

____

Where did drift continue?

____

Did the person apply the standard without waiting for my direction?
Yes / No / Partially / Not yet tested

What evidence supports that answer?

____

What am I still teaching unintentionally?

What behavior must I model more consistently?

What does this person still need before my direct involvement can decrease?

Part II — Sponsorship

Sponsorship is not encouragement alone.
It is the moment your name becomes part of someone else's access.

Sponsorship Readiness Evidence

Person I am assessing for sponsorship:

Reliability

What evidence shows they keep commitments or renegotiate early?

Clean Communication

What evidence shows they surface risk before others have to ask?

Visible Closure

What evidence shows they make completion and the next step clear?

Coachability

What evidence shows they take correction without defensiveness or turning it into a contest?

Discretion

What evidence shows they can carry trust and sensitive context without leaking either?

Pressure Test

What happens to these five signals when stakes, visibility, or uncertainty increase?

Which readiness signal is strongest?

Which signal remains unproven?

What smaller assignment could test that signal?

What would they need to demonstrate before I could responsibly put my name behind them?

Safe With My Name Check

If I endorsed this person today, what risk would I be taking?

Would that risk be:

Reasonable / Premature / Undisciplined

Why?

What pattern makes me trust or hesitate?

What evidence would move this decision forward responsibly?

If You Want Sponsorship

What evidence am I currently giving to the people whose judgment I need?

What still makes me unsafe with someone else's name?

What specific question should I ask instead of "Will you sponsor me?"

Prompt:
What would you need to see from me before you would be comfortable putting your name behind me for broader work?

Write your version:

Sponsorship Decision

Based on the evidence, I will:

Sponsor now / Test readiness through a smaller assignment / Continue development / Do not sponsor at this time

Why:

____

The evidence supporting this decision:

____

The readiness signal that still needs to be tested:

____

The next opportunity or assignment:

____

The support or guardrail that may be needed:

____

What would confirm that the decision was sound?

____

Scaling Commitment

The standard I will transfer more clearly:

The person I will develop through the next three conversations:

The mentorship behavior I will model consistently:

The drift I will correct more directly:

If I am preparing to sponsor someone:

The person whose readiness I will test:

The evidence I still need:

The next assignment or opportunity I will use:

If I am seeking sponsorship:

The evidence I need to strengthen:

The question I will ask:

The decision or action I will carry into the Final Commitment:

SECTION X — LEGACY CHECK

Legacy is not what people say about you at the end.

It is what your name still produces when you are no longer present to direct the work.

Use this section to test whether your standards, impact, and investment in people and systems can continue without your direct presence.

The Legacy Question

If your name were mentioned five years from now in a room you are not in, what should it trigger?

What should people still be able to count on because of you?

What should remain stronger because you were there?

Titles and Names

What part of my influence currently depends too heavily on title or position?

What part could continue without my direct authority?

What standard do I want to remain when my title is gone?

The Three Components of Legacy

Legacy is built through three reinforcing elements:

Integrity → Impact → Investment

Integrity

Integrity is the standard your name remains trusted for.

What standard do I want my name to remain trusted for?

What behavior proves that standard?

Where does my current behavior weaken that standard?

Impact

Impact is the value your work continues to create.

What value do I want my work to keep creating?

Who or what currently benefits from that value?

What evidence would show that this impact continues without me?

Investment

Investment is the people and systems prepared to carry that value forward.

Who or what is currently prepared to carry that value forward?

Where is that transfer already visible?

Where does it still depend too heavily on my presence?

What Your Name Is Teaching Now

What do people currently learn from my example?

Circle any that apply:

Clarity / Ownership / Reliability / Calm under pressure / Truthfulness / Clean finish / Development of others / Discretion / Delay / Reactivity / Inconsistency / Avoidance

What am I teaching clearly?

What am I teaching unintentionally?

What behavior have I allowed that I would not want repeated after me?

What behavior do I most want others to continue because they experienced it from me?

The Legacy Standard

What is the one behavior I want my name to keep teaching long after my role changes?

Why does that behavior matter?

What would prove that this standard is actually transferring?

Legacy Transfer Test

Review one standard, one person, and one system that should remain strong without your direct presence.

The Standard

The standard I want to continue:

What evidence shows that others understand it?

What evidence shows that others can apply it without me?

Where does the standard still depend on my presence?

The Person

The person most likely to carry this standard:

What have they already demonstrated?

What decision can they make without waiting for me?

What development, correction, or opportunity do they still need?

The System

The process, rhythm, practice, or guardrail that should reinforce this standard:

What currently works?

What would weaken if I left today?

What handoff, guardrail, or operating rhythm is still missing?

The Evidence

What would prove that the standard is becoming durable?

What should remain stronger six months after my role changes?

Legacy Check

If I left my current role today, what would likely continue because of me?

What would likely weaken or disappear?

What does that reveal?

Current Legacy State

Based on the evidence, my influence is:

Presence-dependent / Partially transferred / Becoming durable

Why:

____

The most consequential dependency that remains:

____

What would move my influence to the next level of durability?

____

Carry Forward

The standard I will make more transferable:

____

The person I will prepare to carry it:

____

The system or process I will strengthen:

____

The behavior I will model more consistently:

____

The behavior I will stop tolerating:

____

The first action I will take:

____

By when:

____

The evidence I expect to see:

____

The commitment I will carry into the Final Commitment:

____

FINAL COMMITMENT

The value of this workbook is not in what you wrote once. It is in what you now choose to repeat.

Use this final section to turn what you have learned into one visible operating commitment for the next 30 days. Keep it simple, specific, and behavioral. The goal is not to change everything at once. It is to choose the pattern that would most strengthen what your name teaches others to expect, then repeat it long enough to create new evidence.

Choose the Commitment

Review the corrections, decisions, and carry-forward actions you identified throughout the workbook.

The pattern that most needs to change:

____

The evidence that led me to this conclusion:

____

The section where this became clearest:

The Name Test / Define Your Brand Worth / Brand Worth Equation / Reliability / Pressure / Failure / Communication / Consistency / Mentorship & Sponsorship / Legacy

The one commitment that would most strengthen what my name teaches others to expect:

____

One Operating Behavior

What is the one behavior I will reinforce whenever the relevant moment appears during the next 30 days?

When and where should this behavior appear?

What trigger should remind me to use it?

What old behavior will it replace?

Why this behavior matters to my Brand Worth:

One Non-Negotiable Standard

What is the one standard I will not compromise, even under pressure?

What does that standard look like in behavior?

Under what condition is this standard hardest for me to hold?

What will I do when that condition appears?

One Signal

When my name comes up, what signal do I most want it to create?

What repeated evidence will make that signal believable?

What would show me that other people are beginning to experience this signal?

30-Day Action Plan

For the next 30 days, I will:

I will begin on:

The people most likely to experience the difference:

The behavior, result, or operating difference they should notice:

The evidence I will collect:

The person who can give me honest feedback:

I will review the evidence on:

Day 7 / Day 14 / Day 21 / Day 30

I will know the pattern is changing when:

If the pattern breaks, I will:

Final Check

At the end of 30 days, ask:

What did my behavior teach people to expect from my name?

What became more trustworthy, usable, or dependable?

What did others stop having to chase, verify, or compensate for?

Did the signal attached to my name begin to change?

Yes / No / Partially / Not yet clear

What evidence supports that answer?

What still needs correction?

My next decision:

Continue this commitment / Refine this commitment / Choose a new correction

The behavior I will carry forward:

Closing Standard

Your name becomes valuable through repeated evidence. Not one strong day. Not one good intention. Not one polished impression. What you choose next, and what you repeat after that, is what your name will carry.

Closing — Your Name Opens Doors

Your name will continue entering rooms before you do.

It will enter meetings, recommendations, assignments, opportunities, and decisions where you are not present to explain your intentions. It will arrive carrying evidence: the trust you have earned, the consistency you have demonstrated, the results you have delivered, and the standards people have learned to associate with you.

That evidence will either reduce hesitation or create it. It will either make the next decision easier or make the room reach for more protection. It will either open access or narrow it quietly before anything formal is said.

That is the responsibility of Brand Worth.

Your name is not built by what you hope people believe. It is built by the pattern your behavior makes difficult to ignore. Every commitment, update, handoff, recovery, and decision teaches people what to expect. Over time, those lessons gather. They become expectation. They become trust or caution. They become the meaning attached to your name.

The work is not to manage perception after doubt has formed. The work is to build evidence strong enough that confidence arrives before explanation is required.

The work begins in ordinary places: a clearer commitment, earlier updates, cleaner finishes, steadier responses under pressure, and more honest recovery after failure.

It extends through standards transferred to others, endorsements given with discipline, and systems strengthened enough to continue without you.

These are not small things. They are the material from which Brand Worth is built. The question is not whether your name will carry meaning. It already does. The question is whether that meaning will be accidental or intentional.

If your name opens a door, let it be because your pattern has earned the trust behind it. Let it be because your work makes decisions clearer, responsibilities easier to entrust, and people stronger. Let it be because the standard attached to your name has become useful beyond your presence.

That is the work of Reputation and the discipline of Brand Worth: **building a name that opens doors before you ever enter the room.**

THE FOUNDRY PRESS

The Foundry Press is the publishing imprint of QTR Foundry. We publish practical leadership books for people responsible for decisions, teams, systems, and results in complex environments.

Our work is built around a simple premise: leadership begins to weaken where intent, behavior, and execution stop aligning. That is where our books operate. Each title helps leaders think more clearly, act with greater discipline, and build standards that hold under pressure. The goal is not inspiration without application, but usable judgment, sharper behavior, and better execution.

The QTR Foundry Leadership System is organized around four connected phases—Intentionality, Reputation, Execution, and Stewardship. Together, they describe how leadership matures: from self-command to earned trust, from earned trust to disciplined action, and from disciplined action to multiplied value through other people. The Foundry Press gives that progression practical form through books leaders can return to, teach from, and use in the work.

This is not theory detached from practice. It is forged in the realities of leadership under pressure.

Learn more: **qtrfoundry.com**

TAKE THIS FURTHER

If this book gave language to patterns you have already seen, do not let the work stop at agreement. Brand Worth is built by applying the system where trust, pressure, communication, and execution are already shaping results. The real test is not whether the system makes sense. It is whether your behavior changes what your name carries.

QTR Foundry works with leaders, teams, and organizations that need to reduce uncertainty, strengthen execution, and build leadership standards that hold under pressure. We help leaders identify the real source of friction, strengthen trust and accountability, improve decision discipline, and create operating patterns people can rely on.

At the organizational level, Brand Worth becomes a way to read the operating signals behind execution. It reveals the patterns behind execution drag, communication breakdowns, unclear ownership, decision hesitation, and uneven trust. Those signals show where confidence is building, where capacity is leaking, and where execution is slowing before the damage appears in traditional performance metrics.

Depending on the need, the work may take the form of a focused executive session, a team-based leadership lab, or a sustained advisory partnership. The form may change. The purpose does not: turn leadership standards into operating behavior people can rely on.

If your organization is dealing with unclear ownership, slow decisions, uneven trust, communication breakdowns, or execution that depends too heavily on a few individuals, this work can help. QTR Foundry helps leaders turn those signals into clearer decisions, stronger accountability, and more dependable execution.

To bring QTR Foundry into your organization:

qtrfoundry.com
twigington@qtrfoundry.com

WHERE TO GO NEXT

You have now completed the Reputation phase of the QTR Foundry Leadership System. You have seen how trust, consistency, and delivered results shape what your name carries before you speak—and how that Brand Worth influences confidence, access, and opportunity.

But Reputation is not the final step. Once your name carries trust, the next question becomes whether you can use that trust to move work forward without creating chaos.

Continue with ***Running With Scissors***, the Execution phase of the QTR Foundry Leadership System. It moves leadership from trusted reputation to disciplined action under pressure: sharpen the idea before motion, cut unnecessary complexity, establish guardrails, protect the people doing the work, and execute without turning urgency into chaos. Trust gives you room to move. Execution determines whether you use that room well.

Then continue with ***Stewards Not Gatekeepers***, the Stewardship phase. It moves leadership beyond your own performance and into responsibility for people, systems, and standards. The test is whether you can develop others, extend trust without lowering the standard, and build systems that multiply leadership instead of bottlenecking it. Influence without stewardship is incomplete.

Together, the four books form one operating sequence. *On Purpose* builds Intentionality. ***Your Name Opens Doors*** builds Reputation. ***Running With Scissors*** builds Execution. ***Stewards Not Gatekeepers*** builds Stewardship. Leadership is built through intention, proven through reputation, tested through execution, and multiplied through stewardship. That is the QTR Foundry standard.

The four-book pathway is the first operating sequence within a broader QTR Foundry leadership architecture. That larger progression follows six stages: Identity, Trust, Execution, Transformation, Judgment, and Legacy.

The two structures serve different purposes. The four-book pathway gives leaders the core operating sequence of Intentionality, Reputation, Execution, and Stewardship. The six-stage progression shows how the work expands through additional developmental stages and titles. Figure 12 places ***Your Name Opens Doors*** within that broader architecture.

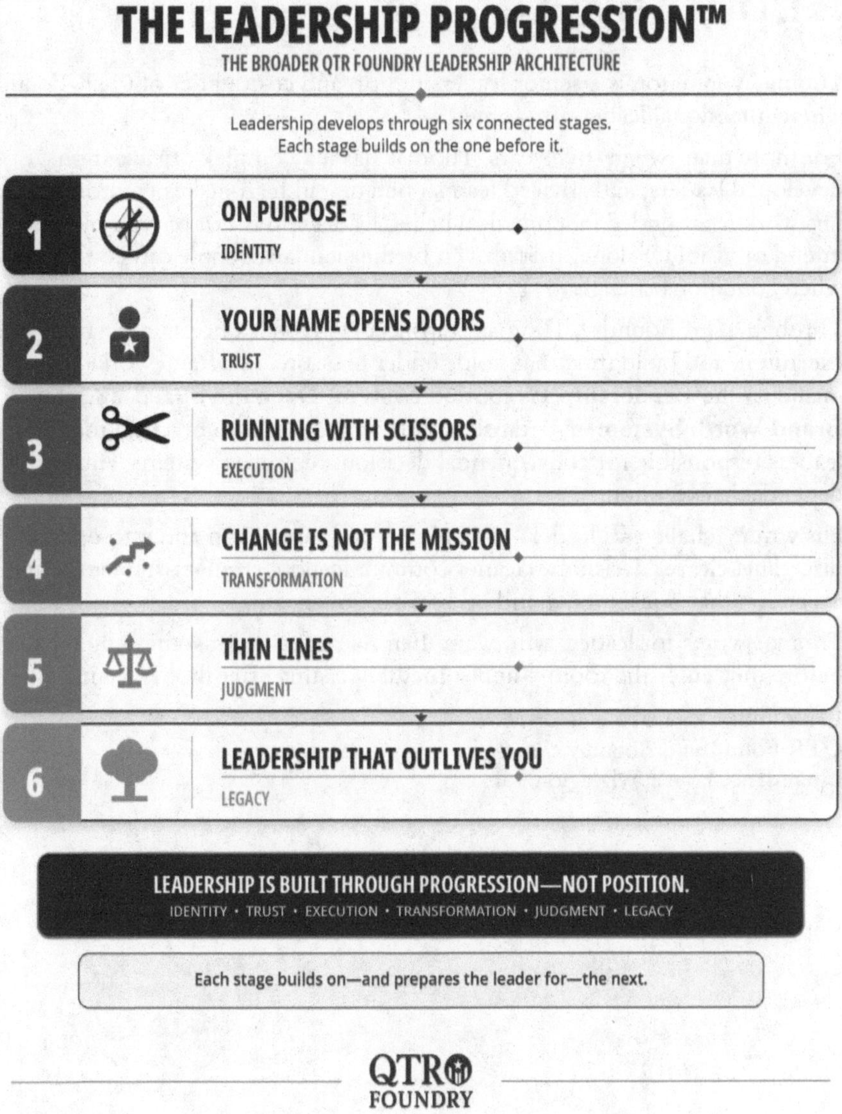

Figure 12 — The Leadership Progression

The broader QTR Foundry leadership architecture. Leadership develops through Identity, Trust, Execution, Transformation, Judgment, and Legacy. Each stage builds on the one before it.

About the Author

Thomas Wigington is a senior leader, author, and co-founder of QTR Foundry, where intentional leaders are forged.

For more than twenty-five years, Thomas has led complex organizations, developed leaders, and advised teams operating in high-stakes environments. His work is grounded in a practical belief: leadership is not proven by title, intent, or visibility alone. It is proven by the standard people can count on when conditions change.

Through QTR Foundry, Thomas helps leaders reduce uncertainty, strengthen execution, and build trust that holds under pressure. His frameworks—including the **Leadership Execution System**, **Decision Space**, and the **Brand Worth System™**—translate those principles into practical tools for leaders responsible for consequential decisions, complex systems, and dependable execution.

His writing challenges leaders to move beyond inspiration and into operating discipline: clearer decisions, cleaner communication, stronger standards, and execution that does not depend on constant oversight.

Thomas writes for leaders who want their names to mean something reliable before they enter the room—and something lasting after they leave it.

Learn more: thomaswigington.com
QTR Foundry: qtrfoundry.com
LinkedIn: Thomas Wigington

www.ingramcontent.com/pod-product-compliance
Lightning Source LLC
LaVergne TN
LVHW041207061126
851857LV00018B/1973
* 9 7 9 8 9 9 5 6 9 3 9 5 6 *